THE GARDEN OF THEOPHRASTUS

PETER HUCHEL

The Garden of Theophrastus & Other Poems

translated by
MICHAEL HAMBURGER

CARCANET NEW PRESS / MANCHESTER
RAVEN ARTS PRESS / DUBLIN

Copyright © The Estate of Peter Huchel (Poems) 1983
Copyright © Michael Hamburger (Translations) 1983
For the poems from *Die Sternenreuse (Gedichte)*:
© R. Piper & Co Verlag, München 1967, 1983
For the poems from *Chausseen Chausseen*: © S. Fischer Verlag,
Frankfurt am Main, 1963
For the poems from *Gezählte Tage*: © Suhrkamp Verlag,
Frankfurt am Main, 1972
For the poems from *Die neunte Stunde*: © Suhrkamp Verlag,
Frankfurt am Main, 1979

All Rights Reserved

First published in 1983 by

Carcanet New Press Ltd   Raven Arts Press
210 Corn Exchange Buildings   31 North Frederick St
Manchester M4 3BQ   Dublin 1

Huchel, Peter
The garden of Theophrastus & other poems
I. Title
831'.914   PR2617.U3

ISBN 0-85635-418-X (Carcanet)
ISBN 0-906897-59-9 (Raven Arts)

Carcanet New Press Ltd., acknowledges the financial assistance of the
Arts Council of Great Britain.
Raven Arts Press acknowledges the financial assistance of the
Arts Council of Ireland (An Chonhairle Ealaion, Dublin).

Printed in England by SRP Ltd., Exeter

CONTENTS

Introduction 9

From *GEDICHTE (1948)*
Die Magd /The Maid 18/19
Der polnische Schnitter/The Polish Reaper 22/23
Sommer/Summer 24/25
Deutschland/Germany...........................26/27

From *CHAUSSEEN CHAUSSEEN (1963)*
Das Zeichen/The Sign 30/31
Landschaft hinter Warschau
    /Landscape beyond Warsaw..................32/33
Elegie/Elegy 34/35
Thrakien/Thrace 36/37
Monterosso/Monteroso 38/39
San Michele/San Michele........................40/41
Ferme Thomasset/Ferme Thomasset...............42/43
Wei Dun und die alten Meister
    /Wei Dun and the Old Masters................44/45
Unter der Kiefer/Under the Pine Tree..............48/49
Auffliegende Schwäne/Swans Rising...............48/49
Hinter den Ziegelöfen/Behind the Brick Kilns........50/51
Chausseen/Roads...............................50/51
Der Treck/The Trek 52/53
Die Pappeln/The Poplars.........................54/55
Winterquartier/Winter Billet 58/59
Polybios/Polybios 60/61
An taube Ohren der Geschlechter
    /To the Deaf Ears of the Generations 66/67
Warschauer Gedenktafel/Warsaw Memorial Tablet 68/69
In Memoriam Paul Eluard/In Memoriam Paul Eluard ..68/69
Die Garten des Theophrast
    /The Garden of Theophrastus 70/71
Traum im Tellereisen/Dream in the Steel Trap 70/71
Psalm/Psalm 72/73

From GEZÄHLTE TAGE (1972)

Ophelia/Ophelia 76/77
Antwort/Answer 78/79
Ankunft/Arrival 80/81
Exil/Exile 82/83
'Die Gaukler sind fort'/'The jugglers have gone' 84/85
Venedig im Regen/Venice in Rain.................86/87
Gezählte Tage/Days that are Numbered 88/89
Die Wasseramsel/The Water Ousel.................90/91
Auf den Tod von V. W./On the Death of V. W........90/91
Der Schlammfang/The Mudcatchers 92/93
Middleham Castle/Middleham Castle...............94/95
Macbeth/Macbeth 96/97
Die Nachbarn/My Neighbours....................98/99
Die Engel/The Angels 100/101
'Unter der blanken Hacke des Monds'
 /'Under the moon's bright mattock..........102/103
'Gehölz'/'Spinney'.............................102/103
April '63/April '63 ....104/105
Meinungen/Opinions...........................106/107
Pe-Lo-Thien/Pe-Lo-Tien 108/109
'Am Tage meines Fortgehns'
 /'This day of my going'...................110/111
Hubertusweg/The Street 112/113
Unkraut/Weeds 116/117
Das Gericht/The Law Court 118/119

DIE NEUNTE STUNDE (1979)

'Der Holunder'/'The elder tree'.................122/123
Der Ammoniter/The Ammonite 124/125
Melpomene/Melpomene 126/127
Das Grab des Odysseus/The Grave of Odysseus.....128/129
Pfeilspitze des Ada/Ada's Arrowhead 130/131
Aristeas I/Aristeas I..........................132/133
Aristeas II/Aristeas II 134/135
Begegnung/Meeting............................136/137
Wintermorgen in Irland/Winter Morning in Ireland ..138/139
Jan-Felix Caerdal/Jan-Felix Caerdal 140/141

In Memoriam Günter Eich
   /In Memoriam Günter Eich 142/143
Philipp/Philip 142/143
Friede/Peace 144/145
Schottischer Sommer/Scottish Summer 144/145
In Bud/At Bud 146/147
Znorovy/Znorovy 148/149
Die neunte Stunde/The Ninth Hour 150/151
Blick aus dem Winterfenster
   /View from the Winter Window 150/151
Östlicher Fluss/Eastern River 152/153
Mein Grossvater/My Grandfather 154/155
Die Katze/The Cat 156/157
Brandenburg/Brandenburg 156/157
Unterwegs/On the Way 158/159
Entzauberung/The Spell Breaks 160/161
Bretonischer Klostergarten
   /Breton Monastery Garden 162/163
Ein Toscaner/A Tuscan 162/163
Rom/Rome 164/165
Persephone/Persephone 164/165
Nachts/By Night 166/167
Die Rückkehr/The Return 168/169
Der Ketzer aus Padua/The Heretic from Padua 170/171
'Nichts...'/'Nothing...' 174/175
Im Kun-Lun-Gebirge/In the Kun-Lun Mountains . . . 176/177
König Lear/King Lear 180/181
'Im Kalmusgeruch'/'In the rush odour' 182/183
Todtmoos/Todtmoos 182/183
'Der Fremde'/'The stranger' 182/183

INTRODUCTION

PETER HUCHEL's whole working life was a struggle for continuity and independence, against the strongest pressures from all sides to break the continuity by committing himself to this line or that, this or that political cause or party, this or that literary group or trend. At the cost of producing no more than four books of poems in a working life more than half a century long—at the cost of silence, exile, and a cunning that consisted in avoiding outward commitments so as to remain true to his inward one—he came through, integral and intact, whatever compromises may have been imputed to him by his critics in either Germany. Those seeming compromises, too, were outward ones, imposed on him by the need to keep going somehow in the thick of the corporative manias of his time, or by hopes briefly shared with the makers of history, but abandoned as soon as they had proved vain.

Huchel's early poems, written in the 1920s and 1930s, were celebrations of rural life, markedly regional in imagery and diction. It was their realism, their earthiness and wealth of observed, lived particulars—already combined with religious, mythical and occult overtones and undertones—that set them apart from the general run of post-Romantic 'nature poetry'. Nor, in those poems, was nature ever an alternative to human and social concerns, let alone an escape from civilization and its discontents—as in some of the new nature poetry produced by other Germans in those highly politicized decades. These early poems of Huchel's did not fit into any of the movements or schools so dear to German historians of literature, including contemporary literature, and Huchel's name is not to be found in most of the standard surveys of German literature published before 1950. After the various modernist movements, of which Expressionism was the most pervasive in the German-speaking countries, their tight formal structure made Huchel's early poems look like a reversion to older traditions of lyrical verse. Yet Huchel had assimilated Expressionist practices, as the syntax of his early poems shows. Despite their realism, these poems also differed from the mundane, up-to-date and colloquial manner of the 'Neue Sachlichkeit'—the New Objectivity—that was a reaction to the emotive excesses of late Expressionism, for they were poems of personal experience as much as of social comment. To a most uncommon degree, in a period of various sorts of alienation, the person of these poems was identified with a specific community, a specific way of life, and the values that had sustained them. Since these values were already threatened, economically, politically and ideologically, Huchel's early celebrations of the rural poor—of maidservants, coachmen, tinkers and farm labourers, not excluding the migrant foreign labourers employed by Prussian landowners at the time—both anticipate and connect with Huchel's later, mainly elegiac, evocations of the most diverse cultures and ways of life. His regional concerns were to expand well beyond their point of departure; yet that first and first-hand experience of rural life within a single Brandenburg landscape impressed itself so deeply as to provide him with recurrent images for a lifetime, no matter where his later poems were written or set. As Martin Dodsworth noticed in a perceptive review of Huchel's *Selected Poems*, the 'North German landscape of grey plains, water, mists, rain and snow' is 'so deeply part of Huchel's being that even in Venice he sees only the sullen qualities of home, not the "marble forests" or "the silver beaks rising and crossing" but a place where "rain opens pores in the water" '.

Politically, too, the early poems did not fit in. 'The Polish Reaper', for instance, reads like an undisguised call to revolution, but in terms of Huchel's own persistent vision of a good society, not of ideologies widely current then or now. Huchel's very persona in this poem, a foreign worker, removed his poem from any possible proximity to the 'blood and soil' cult that became part of the mystique of National Socialism. Huchel was closer at that time to Marxism, but he never joined the Communist Party or the League of Proletarian Revolutionary Writers, vociferous at that time in its advocacy of 'committed' literature. Not Karl Marx but Joan of Arc is the revolutionary paragon in Huchel's three poems on Germany (translated here from the revised version in the volume of Huchel's collected poems *Gedichte*, published in the 1970s). Closely identified though he was with the exploited and oppressed, Huchel did not regard it as the business of poetry to draw up programmes for political action. The two lines in 'The Polish Reaper' that do seem to call for such action stand out not only from that poem but from the whole body of Huchel's early poetry. In his later work, too, Huchel's commitment rarely becomes explicit. What conveys it to the reader is not plain statement but images, situations, figures in a landscape or interior.

*

Peter Huchel was born into a middle-class family in a suburb of Berlin, Lichterfelde, in 1903, but spent his formative childhood years at his grandfather's farm at Alt-Langewisch in rural Brandenburg. His thorough-going transference of allegiance and affection to the rural environment was enacted most powerfully in his poem on the maidservant who became more than a mother to him. She occurs in other early poems that proved even less translatable. (If my rendering of 'The Maid' is slightly less specific than the original, it is because for once a German poem packed so much significant detail into regular, strictly lyrical stanzas that English could not match its compactness and density. The 'paraffin lamp' of the original had to be reduced to an 'oil lamp', half-rhymes substituted for full ones. The nanny-goat's 'teats', on the other hand, became an 'udder', for the rhythm's sake, though it is the 'teats' that associate the animal with the woman in a marvellously physical and sensuous poem.)

After studying philosophy and German literature at the universities of Berlin, Freiburg and Vienna, Huchel worked in France as a farm labourer and writer, also travelling in the Balkans and in Turkey. After his return to Germany he lived in Berlin, writing radio plays never yet collected in book form. From 1940 to 1945 he served as a soldier, but deserted in 1945. After brief imprisonment in the Soviet Union, he worked as artistic director of the Berlin Radio until 1948. From 1949 to 1962 he edited the East German periodical *Sinn und Form*, settling at Wilhelmshorst near Potsdam. Under his editorship this distinguished literary magazine published contributions by non-Communist writers, both German and foreign, and two special issues devoted to unpublished work by Bertolt Brecht.

For a few years after his return to Germany from the war Huchel set his hopes on the programme of land reform carried out in East Germany and elsewhere. During those years he worked on the longer verse sequences 'Das Gesetz' ('The Law') and 'Malaya', coming closer than in any earlier phase to the didacticism of 'socialist realism' approved by the East German régime. The sequences remained unfinished, and were rejected by Huchel for his collections. His first collection of poems, *Der Knabenteich*, had been ready for publication in 1932, and was awarded a prize in typescript; but Huchel withdrew it before its publication, when the National Socialists had come to power. His early poems were not to be collected until 1948, when his volume *Gedichte* appeared both in East and West Germany.

In 1962 Huchel was removed from his editorship, publicly censured and disgraced, and driven into complete retirement in his house near Potsdam. His next collection could be published only in West Germany, fifteen years after the first; and his later books, too, have appeared only in West Germany. In 1971—after much pressure from the West and an attempt to ransom him from a régime that had no more use for him in any capacity—Huchel was allowed to leave the GDR with his wife and son, at first for Italy, moving on to West Germany, where he settled in a borrowed house at the edge of the Black Forest. Between 1972 and 1977 Huchel travelled widely and intensively as a reader of his poems, and was awarded a succession of prizes for his work. In 1972 he came to London as the Federal Republic's representative at the Fanfare for Europe reading, and returned in 1973 and 1974, with a tour of universities in England, Scotland and Ireland. In 1977 serious illness left him unable to write or travel. A planned and eagerly awaited book of memoirs remained largely unwritten. He died in 1980.

*

The present, much enlarged, selection from Huchel's poetry includes only a few of the poems written before 1948—all I was able to translate—but substantial portions of the second and third collections, and the whole of the fourth and last. Although sneers about an alleged 'international style' in poetry usually arise from ignorance or bigotry—and even if there were such a style, Huchel's poetry would not conform to it any more than to other conventions—it is undeniable that certain modes of free verse are much more amenable to faithful translation than the rhymed, metrical verse, at once close to a tradition and highly individual, of Huchel's most characteristic early poems. His regional ties in those poems, often evident in his choice of words, proved an additional obstacle.

Certainly it was not a desire to be internationally acceptable that impelled Huchel to abandon regular stanza forms in his later poems. He has always been singularly indifferent to the reception of his work, singularly reluctant to issue it at all in book form. (Even his last collection of poems was withdrawn by him for a while when due to be published, and considerably delayed. Most of his writings remain unpublished and uncollected; and his reticence about himself, so essential to his work as to look like a principle, caused him to put off the writing of his memoirs when urged to do so by his publisher.) The rhymed stanzas of his early poems drew their strength from his rootedness. Once that rootedness was disturbed, as it had to be if Huchel was to outgrow his childhood and its pastoral world—obsolescent even when he celebrated it—a corresponding formal development was called for. Only free verse, mastered and modulated with exceptional skill, enabled him to range as widely over history, legend and literature as his later poetry ranges thematically; because rhythmically, too, such free verse can draw on the most various sources and exemplars. Not that Huchel regarded himself as an intellectual or erudite poet. Immediate experience and observation are as operative in his later poems as in the early ones, though the sheer sensuousness of his early response to the 'ten thousand things' of nature gave way to a sparer, more elliptical and allusive evocation of them.

Yet, from the first, Huchel was never content to capture immediate experience. Amongst other things, the whole corpus of his poetry amounts to an imaginative autobiography, a bearing witness to the history whose participant and victim he was; but always with as little emphasis as possible on the merely personal and circumstantial data for their own sake. Not confession, but bearing witness has been his constant aim. Nor is there any real distinction between poems with an unmistakably topical setting—like those about the end of the Second World War, the retreat of soldiers and civilians from the Eastern provinces, or those about Huchel's period of virtual house arrest in the GDR—and poems, like the Shakespearean ones, about historical or mythical figures. The Ophelia of Huchel's poem is as much his own—a victim of the political division of Germany—as Shakespeare's, and the same is true of his ancient Chinese, ancient Greek, or mediaeval figures. Whatever the seeming subject of a poem, Huchel is always concerned with the recurrent processes of nature and with human life in relation to those processes. Deliberate anachronism and shifts of scene in some of the later poems serve to make that connection between different civilizations and ages.

If many of the later poems are also cryptic—essentially and necessarily so—it is because Huchel feels that nature speaks to human beings only in signs and ciphers—like the symbols of myths, which he relates to natural phenomena—and that even a lifetime's attention to those signs does not permit an unambiguous interpretation. This awareness of an incommunicable residue in all communication, to be hinted at between the lines of a poem, never explained or resolved into speculation, becomes most striking in Huchel's third and fourth collections. Yet even in his second collection, which contains the highest proportion of poems that can be read as direct reports on experience, Huchel finds wisdom in the silence of cats, rather than in the 'opinions' too readily offered by his human companions.

For similar reasons, Huchel's work contains very few direct professions of religious faith, though religious preoccupations are implicit in all his work, beginning with the maidservant's whispered prophecies in the early poem, bound up as they are with the lovingness that is her main attribute. Those chiliastic proclivities are shared by the grandfather to whom Huchel devoted a poem in his last book, and intimations of them are never wholly absent from Huchel's work. The predominance of elegy and lament in the later work is Huchel's response to the facts of history, to violence, cruelty, intolerance and destructiveness, as experienced by him directly or by imaginative exploration of the past, but the same vision implies a constant adherence to the alternative, the good society that would not need to be

> *eagerly bent*
> *on self-extinction.*

Michael Hamburger
Suffolk

from
GEDICHTE
(1948)

DIE MAGD

Wenn laut die schwarzen Hähne krähn,
vom Dorf her Rauch und Klöppel wehn,
rauscht ins Geläut rehbraun der Wald,
ruft mich die Magd, die Vesper hallt.

Klaubholz hat sie im Wald geknackt,
die Kiepe mit Kienzapf gepackt.
Sie hockt mich auf und schürzt sich kurz,
schwankt barfuss durch den Stoppelsturz.

Im Acker knarrt die späte Fuhr.
Die Nacht pecht schwarz die Wagenspur.
Die Geiss, die zottig mit uns streift,
im Bärlapp voll die Zitze schleift.

Ein Nussblatt wegs die Magd zerreibt,
dass grün der Duft im Haar mir bleibt.
Riedgras saust grau, Beifuss und Kolk.
Im Dorf kräht müd das Hühnervolk.

Schon klinkt sie auf das dunkle Tor.
Wir tappen in die Kammer vor,
wo mir die Magd, eh sie sich labt,
das Brot brockt und den Apfel schabt.

Ich frier, nimm mich ins Schultertuch.
Warm schlaf ich da im Milchgeruch.
Die Magd ist mehr als Mutter noch.
Sie kocht mir Brei im Kachelloch.

Wenn sie mich kämmt, den Brei durchsiebt,
die Kruke heiss ins Bett mir schiebt,
schlägt laut mein Herz und ist bewohnt
ganz von der Magd im vollen Mond.

Sie wärmt mein Hemd, küsst mein Gesicht
und strickt weiss im Petroleumlicht.
Ihr Strickzeug klirrt und blitzt dabei,
sie murmelt leis Wahrsagerei.

THE MAID

When loud in late light black cocks crow,
smoke from the village, clappers blow,
deer-brown the forest's sough blows in,
she calls me, in the church bells' din.

Small kindling in the wood she's cracked,
with pine cones a full basket packed.
Short-hitched, she hoists me up astride,
reels barefoot over stubble field.

Over the field late haywains jar,
night caulks the wheeltracks black as tar.
The shaggy goat that walks with us
drags a full udder through club moss.

She rubs a nut-leaf on her way,
that green in my hair the scent may stay.
Grey roars the sedge, mugwort and pool.
Sleepy the village henfolk call.

She's reached and opened the dark door.
We grope our way across the floor,
the bedroom where, before she eats
my bread she breaks, my apple grates.

I'm cold, so wrap your shawl round me.
Warm there I sleep, milk-fragrantly.
Still more than mother is the maid.
Warm gruel, too, she will provide.

When she combs me or strains the groats,
pushes the hot crock down the sheets,
loudly my heart throbs and contains
only the maid, while the full moon shines.

She warms my shirt, kisses my brow,
whitely knits in the oil-lamp's glow.
Her needles clack and glint, for ease,
gently she murmurs prophecies.

Im Stroh die schwarzen Hähne krähn.
Im Tischkreis Salz und Brot verwehn.
Der Docht verraucht, die Uhr schlägt alt.
Und rehbraun rauscht im Schlaf der Wald.

Up in the straw the black cocks crow.
Faint on the table bread, salt grow.
The low wick smokes, old clock strikes deep.
Deer-brown the forest soughs in sleep. (1931)

DER POLNISCHE SCHNITTER

Klag nicht, goldäugige Unke,
im algigen Wasser des Teichs.
Wie eine grosse Muschel
rauscht der Himmel nachts.
Sein Rauschen ruft mich heim.

Geschultert die Sense
geh ich hinab die helle Chaussee,
umheult von Hunden,
vorbei an russiger Schmiede,
wo dunkel der Amboss schläft.

Draussen am Vorwerk
schwimmen die Pappeln
im milchigen Licht des Mondes.
Noch atmen die Felder heiss
im Schrei der Grillen.

O Feuer der Erde,
mein Herz hält andere Glut.
Acker um Acker mähte ich,
kein Halm war mein eigen.

Herbststürme, weht!
Auf leeren Böden
werden die hungrigen Schläfer wach.
Ich gehe nicht allein
die helle Chaussee.

Am Rand der Nacht
schimmern die Sterne
wie Korn auf der Tenne,
kehre ich heim ins östliche Land,
in die Röte des Morgens.

THE POLISH REAPER

Do not cry, golden-eyed frog,
in the pond's weedy water.
Like a great conch
the night sky roars.
Its roaring calls me home.

My scythe shouldered
I walk down the bright main road,
dogs howling round me,
past the smithy's grime
where darkly the anvil sleeps.

Down by the outwork
poplars are drifting
in the moon's milky light.
Still the meadows exhale heat
in the crickets' screeching.

O fire of the earth,
my heart holds a different glow.
Field after field I mowed,
not one blade was my own.

Blow, autumn gales!
On the bare boards of lofts
hungry sleepers awaken.
Not alone I walk
down the bright main road.

At the rim of night
the stars glitter
like grain on the threshing-floor,
where I go home to the eastern country,
into morning's red light.

SOMMER

O Nüstern des Staubs!
Feuerschlund August,
Teiche schlürfend!

Die schartige Sense
des Winds
glüht im Rohr.

Im knisternden Schatten
brütender Garben
hockt der Sommer,
den nackten Fuss
von Stoppeln rissig.

Dich will ich rühmen,
Erde,
noch unter dem Stein,
dem Schweigen der Welt
ohne Schlaf und Dauer.

SUMMER

O nostrils of the dust!
Fiery maw of August
sucking in ponds!

The wind's
nicked scythe
glows in the reeds.

In the crackling shade
of brooding sheaves
Summer crouches,
his bare foot
ripped by stubble.

You I will praise,
Earth,
under the stone slab even,
the silence of a world
without sleep or permanence.

DEUTSCHLAND

I.
Barg sich auch Feuer und Gold genug
    unter den schweren Wurzeln im Wald,
Deutschland ist dunkel, Deutschland ist kalt.

Wo die Flamme russte im Ring,
    Klebt das Salz der Träne am Krug,
rann durchs Bahrtuch klagend das Blut.

Niemals aber im Frühtau ging,
    hell gerufen von Stimmen stark,
in den Augen gekreuzigte Glut,
    nackten Fusses eine Jeanne d'Arc.   (1927)

II.
Späteste Söhne, rühmet euch nicht,
einsame Söhne, hütet das Licht.
Dass es von euch in Zeiten noch heisst,
dass nicht klirret die Kette, die gleisst,
leise umschmiedet, Söhne, den Geist.   (1933)

III.
Welt der Wölfe, Welt der Ratten.
Blut und Aas am kalten Herde.
Aber noch streifen die Schatten
der toten Götter die Erde.

Göttlich bleibt der Mensch und versöhnt.
Und sein Atem wird frei wieder wehen.
Wenn auch die heulende Rotte höhnt,
sie wird vergehen.   (1939)

GERMANY

I.
Though fire enough lay hidden, and gold,
    under the heavy roots in the wood
Germany's dark, Germany's cold.

Where sooty the flame grew in the ring,
    the salt tears adhered to the pitcher,
blood seeped grievous through the shroud.

But never in the morning dew,
    called by voices strong and stark,
in her eyes the crucified glow,
    barefoot walked a Joan of Arc. (1927)

II.
Latest of sons, do not boast of your might,
lonely sons, take good care of the light.
So that ages to come your name shall inherit,
lest the chain should clank that now gleams bright,
softly cast it, sons, round the spirit. (1933)

III.
World of the wolf, world of the rat.
Blood and carrion on the cold hearth.
But still the dead gods' shadows tread
silently a ravaged earth.

Divine mankind remains, at peace.
And freely again their breath will exhale.
Though now a mocking pack may howl,
it will perish, it will cease. (1939)

from
CHAUSSEEN CHAUSSEEN
(1963)

DAS ZEICHEN

Baumkahler Hügel,
noch einmal flog
am Abend die Wildentenkette
durch wässrige Herbstluft.

War es das Zeichen?
Mit falben Lanzen
durchbohrte der See
den ruhlosen Nebel.

Ich ging durchs Dorf
und sah das Gewohnte.
Der Schäfer hielt den Widder
gefesselt zwischen den Knien.
Er schnitt die Klaue,
er teerte die Stoppelhinke.
Und Frauen zählten die Kannen,
das Tagesgemelk.
Nichts war zu deuten.
Es stand im Herdbuch.

Nur die Toten,
entrückt dem stündlichen Hall
der Glocke, dem Wachsen des Efeus,
sie sehen
den eisigen Schatten der Erde
gleiten über den Mond.
Sie wissen, dieses wird bleiben.
Nach allem, was atmet
in Luft und Wasser.

Wer schrieb
die warnende Schrift,
kaum zu entziffern?
Ich fand sie am Pfahl,
dicht hinter dem See.
War es das Zeichen?

THE SIGN

Hill bare of trees,
once again at evening
the flight of wild ducks passed
through watery autumn air.

Was it the sign?
With pale yellow lances
the lake pierced
unquiet mist.

I walked through the village
and saw what I expected.
The shepherd held a ram
wedged between his knees.
He pared the hoof,
he tarred the stubble lameness.
And women counted the pails,
the day's milking.
There was nothing to interpret.
The accounts had been kept.

Only the dead,
removed from the hourly stroke
of the bell, the ivy's growth,
they see
the icy shadow of earth
slide over the moon.
They know that this will remain.
After all that breathes
in air and water.

Who wrote
the warning words,
hardly to be deciphered?
I found them on the post,
near the lake's far shore.
Was it the sign?

Erstarrt
im Schweigen des Schnees,
schlief blind
das Kreuzotterndickicht.

LANDSCHAFT HINTER WARSCHAU

Spitzhackig schlägt der März
das Eis des Himmels auf.
Es stürzt das Licht aus rissigem Spalt,
niederbrandend
auf Telegrafendrähte und kahle Chausseen.
Am Mittag nistet es weiss im Röhricht,
ein grosser Vogel.
Spreizt er die Zehen, glänzt hell
die Schwimmhaut aus dünnem Nebel.

Schnell wird es dunkel.
Flacher als ein Hundegaumen
ist dann der Himmel gewölbt.
Ein Hügel raucht,
als sässen dort noch immer
die Jäger am nassen Winterfeuer.
Wohin sie gingen?
Die Spur des Hasen im Schnee
erzählte es einst.

Frozen
in the silence of snow
the viper thicket
blindly slept.

LANDSCAPE BEYOND WARSAW

March with its sharp pick
splits the ice of the sky.
From the cracks light pours
billowing down
on the telegraph wires and bare main roads.
At noon white it roosts in the reeds,
a great bird.
When it spreads its claws, brightly
the webs gleam out of thin mist.

Nightfall is brief.
Then more shallow than a dog's palate
the sky arches.
A hill smokes
as though still the huntsmen
were sitting there by the damp winter fire.
Where have they gone?
The hare's tracks in the snow
once told us where.

ELEGIE

Es ist deine Stunde,
Mann auf Chios,
sie naht über Felsen
und legt dir Feuer ans Herz.
Die Abendbrise mäht
die Schatten der Pinien.
Dein Auge ist blind.
Aber im Schrei der Möwe
siehst du metallen schimmern das Meer,
das Meer mit der schwarzen Haut des Delphins,
den harten Ruderschlag des Winds
dicht vor der Küste.

Hinab den Pfad,
wo an der Distel
das Ziegenhaar weht.
Siebensaitig tönt die Kithara
im Sirren der Telegrafendrähte.
Bekränzt von welligen Ziegeln
blieb eine Mauer.
Das Tongefäss zerbrach,
in dem versiegelt
der Kaufbrief des Lebens lag.

Felshohe Gischt,
felsleckende Brandung,
das Meer mit der Haut des Katzenhais.
Am Kap einer Wolke
und in der Dünung des Himmels schwimmend,
weiss vom Salz
verschollener Wogen
des Mondes Feuerschiff.

Es leuchtet der Fahrt nach Ios,
wo am Gestade
die Knaben warten
mit leeren Netzen
und Läusen im Haar.

ELEGY

Your hour it is,
man on Chios,
it comes over rocks
and sets fire to your heart.
The evening breeze mows down
the shadows of pine trees.
Your eye is blind.
But in the gull's cry
you catch the metallic glint of the sea,
the black dolphin-skinned sea,
the wind's hard oar-beat
close to the coast.

Down the path
where on the thistle
goat's hair blows.
The cithara sounds with its seven strings
in the whirr of telegraph wires.
Garlanded with wavy tiles
one wall has remained.
The clay vessel broke
in which, sealed,
lay life's title deed.

Cliff-high breakers,
cliff-licking surf,
the dogfish-skinned sea.
Adrift
round a cloud's cape
and in the sky's swell, white with salt
of waves that receded,
the moon's lightship.

It lights up the crossing to Ios,
where on the shore
wait those boys
with empty nets
and lice in their hair.

THRAKIEN

Eine Flamme züngelt
hier Nachts am Boden,
es wirbelt weisses Laub.
Und mittags zerschellt
die Sichel des Lichts.
Das Rascheln des Sandes
zerklüftet das Herz.

Hebe den Stein nicht auf,
den Speicher der Stille.
Unter ihm
verschläft der Tausendfüssler
die Zeit.

Über den Pass,
gekerbt von Pferdehufen,
weht eine Mähne aus Schnee.
Mit rauchlosen Schatten
vieler Feuer
füllt sich am Abend die Schlucht.

Ein Messer
häutet den Nebel,
den Widder der Berge.
Jenseits des Flusses
leben die Toten.
Das Wort
ist die Fähre.

THRACE

Here a flame licks
the earth by night,
white leafage whirls.
And at noon the sickle
of light shatters.
The rustling of sand
erodes the heart.

Do not lift the stone
that stores up stillness.
Under it
the millipede sleeps away
time.

Over the path
rutted by horses' hooves
blows a mane of snow.
At evening
the gorge fills with the smokeless shadows
of many fires.

A knife
skins the mist,
ram that crops the mountains.
On the other side of the river
the dead live.
What ferries across
is the word.

MONTEROSSO

Aufbrechende Knospe
eines Gitarrenakkords.
Es kündet die Bar
den Abend an.

Auf dem Domplatz
wickelt der Steinmetz
den Meissel ins Tuch.
Turmschwalbenschreie
schleifen die Luft.
Über den Bergen
die Marmorbrüche weisser Wolken,
vom Wind behauen.

Die ihn nicht fanden,
aller Gnaden Quell,
und blieben
beim Angelus
in siebenfacher Schuld,
sie lehnen am Boot
und prüfen
die Schärfe der Harpune.

MONTEROSO

Unfurling bud
of a guitar chord.
The bar announces
evening.

On the cathedral square
the stonemason wraps
up his chisel in cloth.
Crying of swifts
hones the air.
Above the mountains
the marble quarries of white cloud
sculpted by wind.

Those who did not find it,
the fountainhead of all grace,
and at the angelus
remained in a state
of sevenfold sin
rest their backs on the boat-side
and test
the harpoon's sharpness.

SAN MICHELE

Im Mauerwinkel
ein schwarzes Feuer,
den Heimweg der Totan wärmend.
Während der Schatten ihrer Gebete
über schlafende Wasser weht,
schwingt eine Glocke,
die du nicht hörst.
Jede Stunde geht durch dein Herz
und die letzte tötet.

Gestern,
unter den Mandelbäumen,
legten sie Feuer
ans dürre Gras.
Kaufe dich los
im Anblick der Grube.

Die Nacht,
der dunkle Aderlass,
verströmt ins Blei der Dächer.
Das ferne Venedig
ist keinen Fischfang wert.

SAN MICHELE

At the corner of the wall
a black fire
that warms the way home of the dead.
While the shadow of their prayers
wafts over sleeping waters
a bell
you cannot hear swings.
Every hour moves through your heart
and the last kills.

Yesterday,
under the almond trees
they set fire
to the dry grass.
Ransom yourself
in view of the pit.

Night, that dark blood-letting,
seeps into the lead of roofs.
Distant Venice
is not worth a catch of fish.

FERME THOMASSET

Über Stroh und Jauche
das lecke Licht der Stallaterne.
Am Mauerring,
eingemörtelt vom Mond,
das schwere Ochsengeschirr,
die rote Kiefernrute,
das Leder mit tödlichem Bolzen.

Die trübe Stunde,
noch vor dem Fünfuhrmelken—
Es streift
die trockene Blume des Heus
die Trauer breiter Stirnen.

Öffne die Tür.
Es mengt sich der Stalldunst
mit dem milchigen Dinst der Sterne.

Auf den Bergen
die Stille,
vom Fuss der Frühe gekeltert.
Und auf den Steinen,
zertreten,
die weisse Hostie der Apfelblüte.

FERME THOMASSET

Over straw and liquid manure
the stable lamp's leaky light.
On the wall bracket
the moon mortars in,
the heavy ox harness,
the red pine switch,
the leather strap with its deadly bolt.

It's the dim hour
before the five o'clock milking—
the hay's dry flower
grazes
the sadness of wide brows.

Open the door.
The stable fug mingles
with the milky vapour of stars.

On the mountains
a stillness
pressed out by the feet of dawn.
And on the stones,
trampled,
the white Host of apple blossom.

WEI DUN UND DIE ALTEN MEISTER

Bewundernd die alten Meister,
die Steine malten als Knochen der Erde
und dünnen Nebel als Haut der Berge,
war ich bemüht, mit steilem Pinsel,
mit schnellem und verweilendem Strich
den feuchten Glanz des Regens zu tuschen.

Da aber Mond und Sonne beschienen
mehr und mehr verwüstetes Land,
lagen nicht Steine als Knochen der Erde—
Gebein von Menschen knirschte im Sand,
wo Panzer rissen mit fressender Kette
das graue Mark der Strassen bloss.

O alte Meister, ich schabte den Tuschstein.
Ich wusch die Pinsel aus Ziegenhaar.
Doch als ich streifte im Rücken des Feindes,
sah ich die unbewässerten Felder,
das Schöpfrad zerschossen, im harten Geschirr
starr hängen den Ochsen am Göpel,
die Tempelhalle, ausgeplündert,
wo auf dem Schutt lasierter Kacheln
im weissen Mittag die Schlange schlief.

O alte Meister, wie sollte ich tuschen
die felsige Rückenflosse der Flüsse,
als stünde lauernd im flachen Wasser
ein riesiger Fisch mit Kiemen aus Sonne.
Und tuschen den kühlen Duft des Nebels,
das graue Weiss der schwebenden Schneeluft,
als flöge Flaum aus windigem Nest.

Wohin, wohin zog euer Himmel,
in welche Fernen, erlauchte Meister,
der Hauch der Welt, so leicht verwundbar?
Bilder des Schreckens suchten mich heim
und beizten das Auge mit Rauch und Trauer.

WEI DUN AND THE OLD MASTERS

Admiring the old masters
who painted stones as bones of the earth
and thin mist as the skin of mountains,
I endeavoured to trace in Chinese ink,
with a steep brush, with strokes quick
and lasting, the moist gleam of rain.

But because moon and sun shone
on land more and more laid waste,
stones did not lie there as bones of the earth.
Human skeletons grated in sand
where tanks with their devouring tracks
tore down into the marrow of the roads.

Old masters, I scraped the cake of ink.
I washed the goat-hair brushes.
But when I patrolled at the enemy's rear
I saw the paddies unwatered,
the water scoop shot to pieces, the ox
hang stiff on the whim in its hard harness,
the temple hall plundered
where on the rubble of glazed tiles
at noon a serpent slept.

Old masters, how could I paint
the rocky dorsal fins of rivers
as though in their shallow water there lay in wait
a gigantic fish with sunbeam gills.
How paint the cool fragrance of mist,
the grey white of the hovering snow air,
as though fledglings' down whirled from a windy nest.

Where, where, did your heaven go,
into what distance, exalted masters,
the world's breath, so easily damaged?
Visions of horror afflicted me
and corroded my eyes with smoke and sadness.

Wo bist du, »Flötespielender Schiffer«?
Blickst du im Regen den Wildgänsen nach?
Nachts ging ein Klagen über den Fluss.
Es harkte mit qualmendem Ast dein Weib
in Glut und Asche der Bambushütte,
um deinen schwarzen Schädel zu finden.

Und »Alter Mann, heimkehrend vom Dorffest«,
still durch die Kühle fallenden Taus
auf deinem Wasserbüffel reitend,
blieb nicht dein Diener erschrocken stehn
und liess das Leitseil locker schleifen?
Du lenktest den Büffel hinter den Felsen.
Der Feind war schon vor deinem Tor.

Wo ist das »Gehöft am See«, umweht
vom Haar der Gräser und Bäume?
Und wo im Schnee, gefiltert durch Nebel,
das einsame »Dorf im Hochgebirge«?
Suche hinter den Zäunen aus Feuer!
Ausgedörrt hat alles der Krieg
auf dieser Darre des Todes.

Wo sind die Stimmen, das Gonggetöse,
der Duft von Tusche, ihr Dichter und Maler
der »Landschaft mit Gelehrten bevölkert«?
Wie liegt ihr stumm auf blachem Feld,
beraubt der Schuhe, der Amulette
und preisgegeben den Vögeln und Winden.

Himmel und Erde nähren
noch immer die zehntausend Wesen.
Die Knochen modern in der Tiefe.
Der Atem aber steigt in die Höhe
und fliesst als Licht, durch das ihr einst,
o alte Meister, in grosser Ruhe geschritten.

Where are you, Boatman Playing the Flute?
Do you watch wild geese fly off in the rain?
By night a wailing passed over the river.
Your wife with a smoking stick was raking
the embers and ashes of your bamboo hut
to find the black remains of your head.

And, Old Man Returning from the Village Fête,
peacefully riding your water buffalo
through the coolness of falling dew,
did not your servant, startled, stop,
dropping the rope, which trailed loose?
You drove the buffalo behind the rock.
The enemy was already at your door.

Where is the Homestead by the Lake, surrounded
by the blown hair of grasses and trees?
And where in the snow, filtered through mist,
the solitary Village on the High Plateau?
Look behind the fences of fire!
War has parched it all
in this kiln of death.

Where are the voices, the din of gongs,
the scent of ink, you poets and painters
of the Landscape Peopled with Learned Men?
How silent you lie on the fallow field,
robbed of your shoes, of your amulets
and abandoned to the birds and winds.

Heaven and Earth still sustain,
even now, the ten thousand things.
The bones rot where they fell.
But the breath rises up
and flows as the light through which once,
old masters, you walked in great quietude.

UNTER DER KIEFER

Nadeln ohne Öhr,
der Nebel zieht
die weissen Fäden ein.
Fischgräten,
in den Sand gescharrt.
Mit Katzenpfoten
klettert der Efeu
den Stamm hinauf.

AUFFLIEGENDE SCHWÄNE

Noch ist es dunkel, im Erlenkreis,
die Flughaut nasser Nebel
streift dein Kinn. Und in den See hinab,
klaftertief,
hängt schwer der Schatten.

Ein jähes Weiss,
mit Füssen und Flügeln das Wasser peitschend,
facht an den Wind. Sie fliegen auf,
die winterbösen Majestäten.
Es pfeift metallen.
Duck dich ins Röhricht.
Schneidende Degen
sind ihre Federn.

UNDER THE PINE TREE

Needles without eyes.
The mist
threads them with white cotton.
Fish bones
lightly scratched into sand.
With cats' paws
ivy
climbs the trunk.

SWANS RISING

It is dark still, in the alder circle
the wing membrane of wet mist
grazes your chin. And down into the lake,
fathom-deep,
the shadow hangs heavy.

A sudden white,
lashing the water with feet and wings,
fans the wind. They rise,
their winter-evil majesties.
A metallic whish.
Duck your head in the rushes.
Their feathers
are slashing swords.

HINTER DEN ZIEGELÖFEN

Erhabene Helle,
noch zu finden im fauligen Licht
gestauter Wasser. Hinter den Ziegelöfen,
gleisentlang,
die leichte Dünung der Gräser.
Biege das weisse Schilf zurück,
du stehst vor der Furt des Mittags.
Hier wird Gold gewaschen
und auf zerbrochene Ziegel geschüttet.

CHAUSSEEN

Erwürgte Abendröte
stürzender Zeit!
Chausseen. Chausseen.
Kreuzwege der Flucht.
Wagenspuren über den Acker,
der mit den Augen
erschlagener Pferde
den brennenden Himmel sah.

Nächte mit Lungen voll Rauch,
mit hartem Atem der Fliehenden,
wenn Schüsse
auf die Dämmerung schlugen.
Aus zerbrochenem Tor
trat lautlos Asche und Wind,
ein Feuer,
das mürrisch das Dunkel kaute.

Tote,
über die Gleise geschleudert,
den erstickten Schrei
wie einen Stein am Gaumen.
Ein schwarzes
summendes Tuch aus Fliegen
schloss ihre Wunden.

BEHIND THE BRICK KILNS

Noble brightness
to be found in the putrid light
of stagnant water even. Behind the brick kilns,
on either side of the rails,
a dunescape of rippled grasses.
Bend back the white reeds
and you face the ford of noon.
Here gold is washed
and poured over broken bricks.

ROADS

Choked sunset glow
of crashing time.
Roads. Roads.
Intersections of flight.
Cart tracks across the ploughed field
that with the eyes
of killed horses
saw the sky in flames.

Nights with lungs full of smoke,
with the hard breath of the fleeing
when shots
struck the dusk.
Out of a broken gate
ash and wind came without a sound,
a fire
that sullenly chewed the darkness.

Corpses,
flung over the rail tracks,
their stifled cry
like a stone on the palate.
A black
humming cloth of flies
closed over wounds.

DER TRECK

Herbstprunk der Pappeln.
Und Dörfer
hinter der Mauer
aus Hundegeheul,
am Torweg
eingekeilt der Riegel,
das Gold verborgen
im rostigen Eisentopf.

Spät das letzte Gehöft.
Zerschossen trieb die Kettenfähre
den Fluss hinab.

Hier sah ich das Kind,
gebettet
in den kältesten Winkel der Stunde,
aus der Höhle des Bluts
ans Licht zersplitterter Fenster
gestossen.
Das Kind war nahe dem Tag.

Draussen das Wasserloch
ein Klumpen Eis.
Und Männer rissen mit Bajonetten
Fetzen Fleischs
aus schneeverkrustetem Vieh,
schleudernd den Abfall
gegen die graubemörtelte
Mauer des Friedhofs.

Es kam die Nacht
imkrähentreibenden Nebel.
Hart ans Gehöft
auf Krücken kahler Pappeln
Kam die Nacht.

Das Kind sah nicht
die gräberhohle Erde.

THE TREK

Autumn splendour of poplars.
And villages
behind their wall
of dogs' howling,
at the gateway
the bolt wedged fast,
the gold hidden
in a rusted iron pot.

Late, the last homestead.
Shot up, the chain ferry drifted
down the river.

Here I saw the child
bedded
in the hour's coldest corner,
pushed out
from the blood's cavern
to the light of shattered windows.
The child was near to day.

Outside, the waterhole
was a block of ice.
The men with bayonets ripped
slivers of meat
from snow-encrusted cattle,
hurling the offal
at the grey-cemented
churchyard wall.

Night came
in the crow-driving fog.
Right up to the homestead
on the crutches of bare poplars
night came.

The child did not see
grave-hollow earth.

Und nicht den Mond,
der eine Garbe weissen Strohs
auf Eis und Steine warf.
Das Kind war nahe dem Tag.

DIE PAPPELN

Zeit mit rostiger Sense,
spät erst zogest du fort,
den Hohlweg hinauf
und an den beiden Pappeln vorbei.
die schwammen
im dünnen Wasser des Himmels.
Ein weisser Stein ertrank.
War es der Mond, das Auge der Odnis?

Am Gräbergebüsch die Dämmerung.
Sie hüllte ihr Tuch,
aus Gras und Nebel grob gewebt,
um Helme und Knochen.
Die erste Frühe, umkrustet von Eis,
warf blinkende Scherben ins Schilf.
Schweigend schob der Fischer
den Kahn in den Fluss. Es klagte
die frierende Stimme des Wassers,
das Tote um Tote flösste hinunter.

Wer aber begrub sie, im frostigen Lehm,
in Asche und Schlamm,
die alte Fussspur der Not?
Im Kahlschlag des Kriegs glänzt Ackererde,
es drängt die quellende Kraft des Halms.
Und wo der Schälpflug wendet,
die Stoppel stürzt,
stehn auf dem Hang die beiden Pappeln.
Sie ragen ins Licht
als Fühler der Erde.

Did not see the moon that threw
a sheaf of white straw
at ice and stones.
The child was near to day.

THE POPLARS

Time with your rusty scythe,
late you went on your way,
up the narrow path
and past the two poplars.
They swam
in the sky's thin water.
A white stone drowned.
Was it the moon, desolation's eye?

Dusk on the graveside bushes.
It wound its cloth
coarsely woven of grass and mist
around helmets and bones.
The dawn light, encrusted with ice,
threw glinting shards into rushes.
In silence the fisherman pushed
his boat into the river. The water's
freezing voice complained,
bearing corpse after corpse downstream.

But who buried them in the frosty clay,
in ashes and mud,
disaster's old footprints?
Amid the razing impact of war
the ploughed field glistens, the corn blade's power wells up.
And where the paring plough turns,
where stubble falls,
on the slope the two poplars remain.
They loom into light
as the antennae of Earth.

Schön ist die Heimat,
wenn über der grünen Messingscheibe
des Teichs der Kranich schreit
und das Gold sich häuft
im blauen Oktobergewölbe;
wenn Korn und Milch in der Kammer schlafen,
sprühen die Funken
vom Amboss der Nacht.
Die russige Schmiede des Alls
beginnt ihr Feuer zu schüren.
Sie schmiedet
das glühende Eisen der Morgenröte.
Und Asche fällt
auf den Schatten der Fledermäuse.

Lovely our homeland is
when over the green brass disc
of the pond a crane cries
and gold gathers
in October's blue vault;
when corn and milk sleep in the store-room,
the sparks fly up
from night's anvil.
The world's sooty forge
begins to fan its fire.
It beats out
the glowing iron of dawn.
And ash falls
on the shadows of bats.

WINTERQUARTIER

Ich sitze am Schuppen
und öle mein Gewehr.

Ein streunendes Huhn
drückt mit dem Fuss
zart in den Schnee
weltalte Schrift,
weltaltes Zeichen,
zart in den Schnee
den Lebensbaum.

Ich kenne den Schlächter
und seine Art zu töten.
Ich kenne das Beil.
Ich kenne den Hauklotz.

Schräg durch den Schuppen
wirst du flattern,
kopfloser Rumpf,
doch Vogel noch,
der seinen zuckenden Flügel presst
jäh ans gespaltene Holz.

Ich kenne den Schlächter.
Ich sitze am Schuppen
und öle mein Gewehr.

WINTER BILLET

I sit by the shed,
oiling my rifle.

A foraging hen
with her foot imprints
lightly on snow
a script as old as the world,
a sign as old as the world,
lightly on snow
the tree of life.

I know the butcher
and his way of killing.
I know the axe.
I know the chopping-block.

Across the shed
you will flutter,
stump with no head,
yet still a bird
that presses a twitching wing
down on the split wood.

I know the butcher.
I sit by the shed,
oiling my rifle.

POLYBIOS

   I.

Am Abend
ergoss sich ein Blutsturz
aus der Kehle des Himmels.
Es brannte die Luft
den Toten
purpurne Zeichen ein.

Hinter dem Pfahlwerk
brannte von harten
Schreien der Staub.
Sie häuften die Beute.
Nach jedem Gemetzel
verfaulen sie
in ihrer Stärke.

Zerschneiden wird die Nacht
die Sehnen des Ruhms,
erdrosseln das Gelächter,
den Raub aus kalten Händen graben.

Ich ging durch den Steinschlag
roher Worte
und an den Feuergruben vorbei.
Ich ging zu den Stimmen,
die sie nicht hören.

Zerrädert
die Gräberstrasse,
ein Karrenweg fast.
Geköpfte Säulen,
die Schrift verlodert.
Über dem Schutt
verdunkelter Stimmen
der Rauch des Schierlings.
Und nirgends die Tafel:

POLYBIOS

I.

In the evening
a haemorrhage gushed
from the sky's gullet.
The air branded
a purple mark
on to the dead.

Behind the paling
the dust burned
with sharp screams.
They heaped up their prey.
After each massacre
they rot
in their power.

Night will sever
the sinews of glory,
throttle the laughter,
dig the booty from cold hands.

I passed through the rockfall
of rough words
and passed the fiery pits.
I went to the voices
which they do not hear.

The road to the graveyard
was rutted,
a cart track almost.
Beheaded pillars,
the inscriptions burnt out.
Above the rubble
of darkened voices
the hemlock smoke.
And nowhere the tablet:

Hier liegt einer,
der wollte noch singen
mit einer Distel im Mund.

Knisternd fiel die Hitze
aus glühender Pfanne der Nacht.
Nicht im Brunnen der Stern,
die Scherbe leuchtet
dem sinkenden Krug.
Zerschmetterter Mund,
du leuchtest die Finsternis an.

II.

Zerschossene
Schläfe des Dorfs,
noch immer umschwommen
vom Lindenduft.

Die Dächer gerodet,
das Kirchenschiff
ein glosender Spalt.
Es rief aus dem Rauch:
Ein Engel naht
und setzt seinen Fuss
auf meine Wunde.

Vor mir
in schmerzender Helle
die stinkende Wunde der Chaussee,
verkrustet und wieder aufgerissen.
Und Rinder lagen
aufgeblasen
vom Maul der Verwesung.

Aber ich blieb
an diesen Seen,
wo der November
die Pfeile

Here lies one
who would not desist from singing
with a thistle in his mouth.

Crackling, heat fell
from the night's glowing pan.
Not the star in the well,
the shard it is that shines
to the jug going down.
Shattered mouth,
you shine at the darkness.

II.

Bullet-riddled
temple of the village,
still with the linden tree's fragrance
drifting all round it.

The roofs lifted,
the church's nave
a glimmering cleft.
From the smoke a call:
An angel nears
and sets his foot
upon my wound.

In front of me
in painful brightness
the main road's stinking wound,
dried to a crust and torn open again.
And bullocks lay
blown up
by the maw of decay.

But I remained
by the lakes
where November
splinters

im Köcher des Nebels
zersplittert.
Unter dem Himmel
der Eichelhäher
lief ich durch finstere Dörfer,
wo mittags Elias
aus brennendem Ahorn trat.

Funksprüche
durchtickten den Schlaf.
Am Feldrand die Tote,
die Brauen voll Rauhreif,
zwei weisse Ähren
auf der Stirn.
Das öde Gehöft,
ich trank im Schneewind
und spürte das Eis
am Gaumen der Pumpe.

Spät wird es Tag.
Ein Fittich aus Rauch
weht durch den Himmel
der Eichelhäher.
Verwandelt ist
das Wasser der Seen.
Jede Brombeerranke
ein rostiger Stacheldraht.
Stell deine Hunde
vor die Nacht.

the arrows
in the fog's quiver.
Under the jays'
sky
I ran through dark villages
where at noon Elijah
stepped out of burning maples.

Radio messages
ticked through sleep.
At the field's verge the dead woman,
her eyebrows covered with hoarfrost,
two white ears of corn
on her forehead.
The desolate homestead,
in the snow wind I drank
and tasted the ice
on the pump's palate.

Dawn comes late.
A wing of smoke
drifts through the jays'
sky.
Transmuted in
the lakes' water.
Every bramble tendril
a rusty barbed wire.
Put out your watchdogs
against night.

AN TAUBE OHREN DER GESCHLECHTER

Es war ein Land mit hundert Brunnen.
Nehmt für zwei Wochen Wasser mit.
Der Weg ist leer, der Baum verbrannt.
Die Öde saugt den Atem aus.
Die Stimme wird zu Sand
und wirbelt hoch und stützt den Himmel
mit einer Säule, die zerstäubt.

Nach Meilen noch ein toter Fluss.
Die Tage schweifen durch das Röhricht
und reissen Wolle aus den schwarzen Kerzen.
Und eine Haut aus Grünspan schliesst
das Wasserloch,
als faule Kupfer dort im Schlamm.

Denk an die Lampe
im golddurchwirkten Zelt des jungen Africanus:
Er liess ihr Öl nicht länger brennen,
denn Feuer wütete genug,
die siebzehn Nächte zu erhellen.

   *

Polybios berichtet von den Tränen,
die Scipio verbarg im Rauch der Stadt.
Dann schnitt der Pflug
durch Asche, Bein und Schutt.
Und der es aufschrieb, gab die Klage
an taube Ohren der Geschlechter.

TO THE DEAF EARS OF THE GENERATIONS

There was a land with a hundred wells.
Take two weeks' supply of water.
The path is bare, the tree burnt.
The emptiness drains you of breath.
The voice turns to sand
and whirls up and supports the sky
with a column that in turn will be dust.

After miles, a dead river.
Days maraud through the rushes,
ripping wool from their black candles.
And a skin of verdigris closes
the water hole
as though copper rotted there in the mud.

Think of the lamp
in the gold-threaded tent of young Africanus:
he would not let its oil burn any longer,
since fire enough was raging
to light up the seventeen nights.

*

Polybios tells of the tears
that Scipio hid in the city's smoke.
Then the plough cut
through ashes, bones and rubble.
And he who wrote it down passed on the lament
to the deaf ears of the generations.

WARSCHAUER GEDENKTAFEL

I.
Es liessen die Blitze
zerstörter Sommer
die Asche an den Bäumen.
Im Wundmal der Mauer
erscheinen die Toten.
Die schuhlosen Füsse frieren
im Tau der Rosen.

II.
O heiliges Blut,
es brannte
in allen Adern der Stadt.
Ein Wall
wunden Fleisches
war der Mund.
Am Schweigen
hinter den Zähnen
zerbrach das Eisen.

IN MEMORIAM PAUL ELUARD

Freiheit, mein Stern,
nicht auf den Himmelsgrund gezeichnet,
über den Schmerzen der Welt
noch unsichtbar
ziehst du die Bahn
am Wendekreis der Zeit.
Ich weiss, mein Stern,
dein Licht ist unterwegs.

WARSAW MEMORIAL TABLET

I.
The lightning flashes
of summers destroyed
left cinders on the trees.
Where wounds left the wall scarred
the dead appear.
Shoeless feet freeze
in the dew of roses.

II.
O holy blood,
it burned
in all the veins of the city.
A mound
of ripped flesh
the mouth was.
Against the silence
behind the teeth
iron broke.

IN MEMORIAM PAUL ELUARD

Freedom, my star,
not incised in the sky's vault,
above the world's pain
invisible still
you orbit
at the tropic of time.
I know, my star,
your light is on its way.

DIE GÄRTEN DES THEOPHRAST

Meinem Sohn

Wenn mittags das weisse Feuer
der Verse über den Urnen tanzt,
gedenke, mein Sohn. Gedenke derer,
die einst Gespräche wie Bäume gepflanzt.
Tot ist der Garten, mein Atem wird schwerer,
bewahre die Stunde, hier ging Theophrast,
mit Eichenlohe zu düngen den Boden,
die wunde Rinde zu binden mit Bast.
Ein Ölbaum spaltet das mürbe Gemäuer
und ist noch Stimme in heissen Staub.
Sie gaben Befehl, die Wurzel zu roden.
Es sinkt dein Licht, schutzloses Laub.

TRAUM IM TELLEREISEN

Gefangen bist du, Traum.
Dein Knöchel brennt,
zerschlagen im Tellereisen.

Wind blättert
ein Stück Rinde auf.
Eröffnet ist
das Testament gestürzter Tannen,
geschrieben
in regengrauer Geduld
unauslöschlich
ihr letztes Vermächtnis—
das Schweigen.

Der Hagel meisselt
die Grabschrift auf die schwarze Glätte
der Wasserlache.

THE GARDEN OF THEOPHRASTUS

for my Son

When at noon the white fire of verses
flickering dances above the urns,
remember, my son. Remember the vanished
who planted their conversations like trees.
The garden is dead, more heavy my breathing,
preserve the hour, here Theophrastus walked,
with oak bark to feed the soil and enrich it,
to bandage with fibre the wounded bole.
An olive tree splits the brickwork grown brittle
and still is a voice in the mote-laden heat.
Their order was to fell and uproot it,
your light is fading, defenceless leaves.

DREAM IN THE STEEL TRAP

You are caught, dream.
Your ankle sears,
smashed in the steel trap.

Wind turns the page
of a piece of bark.
Opened up
is the testament of fallen spruces,
written
in rain-grey patience
ineffaceable
its last will —
silence.

Hail chisels
the inscription on to the black smoothness
of a puddle.

PSALM

Dass aus dem Samen des Menschen
kein Mensch
und aus dem Samen des Ölbaums
kein Ölbaum
werde,
es ist zu messen
mit der Elle des Todes.

Die da wohnen
unter der Erde
in einer Kugel aus Zement,
ihre Stärke gleicht
dem Halm
im peitschenden Schnee.

Die Öde wird Geschichte.
Termiten schreiben sie
mit ihren Zangen
in den Sand.

Und nicht erforscht wird werden
ein Geschlecht,
eifrig bemüht,
sich zu vernichten.

PSALM

That from the seed of men
no man
and from the seed of the olive tree
no olive tree
shall grow,
this you must measure
with the yardstick of death.

Those who live
under the earth
in a capsule of cement,
their strength is like
a blade of grass
lashed by snow in a blizzard.

The desert now will be history.
Termites with their pincers
write it
on sand.

And no one will enquire
into a species
eagerly bent
on self-extinction.

from
GEZÄHLTE TAGE
(1972)

OPHELIA

Später, am Morgen,
gegen die weisse Dämmerung hin,
das Waten von Stiefeln
im seichten Gewässer,
das Stossen von Stangen,
ein rauhes Kommando,
sie heben die schlammige
Stacheldrahtreuse.

Kein Königreich,
Ophelia,
wo ein Schrei
das Wasser höhlt,
ein Zauber
die Kugel
am Weidenblatt zersplittern lässt.

OPHELIA

Later, next morning,
when the first white light glints,
the wading of gumboots
in shallow water,
the thump of poles,
an order barked out,
they're hoisting the miry
barbed wire net.

No kingdom,
Ophelia,
where a scream
tunnels the water,
a spell
makes the bullet
shatter against a willow leaf.

ANTWORT

Zwischen zwei Nächten
der kurze Tag.
Es bleibt das Gehöft.
Und eine Falle, die uns
im Dickicht der Jäger stellt.

Die Mittagsöde.
Noch wärmt sie den Stein.
Gezirp im Wind,
das Schwirren einer Gitarre
den Hang hinab.

Die Lunte
aus welkem Laub
glimmt an der Mauer.
Salzweisse Luft.
Pfeilspitzen des Herbstes,
Kranichzüge.

Im hellen Geäst
verhallt der Stundenschlag.
Spinnen legen
aufs Räderwerk
die Schleier toter Bräute.

ANSWER

Between two nights
the brief day.
What remains is the homestead.
And a trap the huntsman
set for us in the thicket.

The desert of noon.
Still it warms rock.
A chirping in the wind,
the whir of a guitar
down the slope.

The slow fuse
of withered foliage
glows on the wall.
Salt-white air.
Arrowheads of autumn,
migrating cranes.

In bright boughs
the stroke of the hour subsides.
On the clockwork
spiders lay
the veils of dead brides.

ANKUNFT

Männer mit weissen
zerfetzten Schärpen
reiten am Rand des Himmels
den Scheunen zu,
Einkehr suchend
für eine Nacht,
wo die Sibyllen
wohnen im Staub der Sensen.

Grünfüssig
hängt das Teichhuhn
am Pfahl.
Wer wird es rupfen?
Wer zündet im blakenden Nebel
das Feuer an?
Weh der verlorenen
Krone von Ephraim,
der welken Blume
am Messerbalken der Mähmaschine,
der Nacht
auf kalter Tenne.

Ein Huf
schlägt noch die Stunde an.
Und gegen Morgen
am Himmel ein Krähengeschrei.

ARRIVAL

Men with white
ragged sashes
ride on the rim of the sky
towards the barns,
looking for lodging
for one night,
where the sibyls
live in the dust of scythes.

Green-footed
the moorhen hangs
on the post.
Who will pluck it?
Who in the smoky haze
will light the fire?
Alas for the lost
crown of Ephraim,
the withered flower
on the shaft of a mower's blades,
for the night
on a cold barn floor.

A hoof
still strikes the hour.
And at daybreak
a shrieking of crows in the sky.

EXIL

Am Abend nahen die Freunde,
die Schatten der Hügel.
Sie treten langsam über die Schwelle,
verdunkeln das Salz,
verdunkeln das Brot
und führen Gespräche mit meinem Schweigen.

Draussen im Ahorn
regt sich der Wind:
Meine Schwester, das Regenwasser
in kalkiger Mulde,
gefangen
blickt sie den Wolken nach.

Geh mit dem Wind,
sagen die Schatten.
Der Sommer legt dir
die eiserne Sichel aufs Herz.
Geh fort, bevor im Ahornblatt
das Stigma des Herbstes brennt.

Sei getreu, sagt der Stein.
Die dämmernde Frühe
hebt an, wo Licht und Laub
ineinander wohnen
und das Gesicht
in einer Flamme vergeht.

EXILE

Friends draw near in the evening,
the hills' shadows.
Slowly they cross the threshold,
darken the salt,
darken the bread
and conduct conversations with my silence.

Outside, in the sycamore
the wind stirs:
My sister, the rain water
in her chalky hollow,
captive
she follows the clouds with her gaze.

Go with the wind,
say the shadows.
Summer lays
an iron sickle over your heart.
Go away, before in the sycamore leaf
the stigma of autumn burns.

Be loyal, says the stone.
Dawn
breaks where light and leafage
live intertwined
and vision
is consumed in a flame.

DIE GAUKLER SIND FORT. Sie gingen
lautlos dem weissen Wasser nach.
Der Fähnrich und das Mädchen,
der bucklige Händler mit Ketten und Ringen,
sie alle sind fort.
Es blieb der Hügel,
wo sie sich trafen,
die Eiche, mächtig gegabelt,
in grüner Wipfelwildnis.

Mittags,
unter der Wärme des Steins,
hörst du Orgelklänge,
und eine Maske, maulbeerfarben,
weht durchs Gebüsch.

Die Eiche, mächtig gegabelt,
die den Donner barg—
in morscher Kammer des Baums
schlafen die Fledermäuse,
drachenhäutig.
Die hochberühmten Gaukler sind fort.

THE JUGGLERS HAVE GONE. Noiselessly
they followed the white water.
The ensign and the girl,
the hunchback merchant with chains and rings,
all have gone.
What remains is the hill
where they used to meet,
the oak, hugely forked,
in a green riot of treetops.

At noon,
amid the stone's warmth,
you hear organ strains
and a mask, mulberry-coloured,
is blown through the shrubs.

The oak, hugely forked,
that contained thunder—
in the trunk's dank interior
bats are asleep,
dragon-skinned.
The world-famous jugglers have gone.

VENEDIG IM REGEN

Noch im Nebel
leuchtet das Gold des Löwen,
das steinerne Laubwerk tropft.
Namen, meergeboren,
wer schrieb sie ins salzige Licht?
Keiner nennt
die grosse Geduld
der Pfähle.

Auf die Fähre
wartend im Regen,
der Poren
ins Wasser schlägt,
blick ich hinüber
zu den rostigen Schiffen
der Giudecca.

Die Seekarten schweigen.
Es schweigt
die Muschel
am Nacken des Steins.

VENICE IN RAIN

The gold of the lion shines
even in mist,
the stone leafage drips.
Names born in the sea,
who wrote them into the salty light?
No one mentions
the great patience
of the supporting piles.

Waiting for the ferry
while rain
opens pores
in the water,
I look across
at the rusted boats
of the Giudecca.

The sea charts are silent.
And silent
is the limpet
on the stone's neck.

GEZÄHLTE TAGE

Gezählte Tage, Stimmen, Stimmen,
vorausgesandt durch Sonne und Wind
und im Gefolge rasselnder Blätter,
noch ehe der Fluss
den Nebel speichert im Schilf.

Vergiss die Stadt,
wo unter den Hibiskusbäumen
das Maultier morgens gesattelt wird,
der Gurt gezogen, die Tasche gepackt,
die Frauen stehn am Küchenfeuer,
wenn noch die Brunnen im Regen schlafen.
Vergiss den Weg,
betäubt vom Duft des Pfeifenstrauchs,
die schmale Tür,
wo unter der Matte der Schlüssel liegt.

Zwei Schatten,
Rücken an Rücken,
zwei Männer warten am frostigen Gras.
Stunde,
die nicht mehr deine Stunde ist,
Stimmen,
vorausgesandt durch Nebel und Wind.

DAYS THAT ARE NUMBERED

Days that are numbered, voices, voices,
sent on ahead through sunshine and wind,
in the wake of rattling leaves,
before the river begins
to store up mist in the rushes.

Forget the town
where under hibiscus trees
the mule is saddled each morning,
the girth is tightened, the saddlebag packed,
the women stand by the kitchen fire,
with the wells asleep still in the rain.
Forget the path
dazed by syringa fragrance,
the narrow door
where the key lies under the mat.

Two shadows
back to back,
two men waiting in the rimy grass.
Hour
that is not yours any more,
voices
sent on ahead through mist and wind.

DIE WASSERAMSEL

Könnte ich stürzen
heller hinab
ins fliessende Dunkel

um mir ein Wort zu fischen,

wie diese Wasseramsel
durch Erlenzweige,
die ihre Nahrung

vom steinigen Grund des Flusses holt.

Goldwäscher, Fischer,
stellt eure Geräte fort.
Der scheue Vogel

will seine Arbeit lautlos verrichten.

AUF DEN TOD VON V. W.

Sie vergass die Asche
auf den gekrümmten Tasten des Klaviers,
das flackernde Licht in den Fenstern.

Mit einem Teich begann es,
dann kam der steinige Weg,
der umgitterte Brunnen, von Beifuss bewachsen,
die löchrige Tränke unter der Ulme,
wo einst die Pferde standen.

Dann kam die Nacht,
die wie ein fallendes Wasser war.
Manchmal, für Stunden,
ein Vogelgeist,
  halb Bussard, halb Schwan,
hart über dem Schilf,
aus dem ein Schneesturm heult.

THE WATER OUSEL

If I could swoop
down more brightly
into the flowing dark

to catch myself a word,

like this water ousel
through alder branches
to pick her sustenance

from the stony riverbed.

Goldwashers, fishermen,
put away your gear.
The shy bird

wants to do its work in silence.

ON THE DEATH OF V. W.

She forgot about the ash
on the warped piano keys,
the flickering light in the windows.

It began with a pond,
then came the pebbly path,
the railed well, with mugwort around it,
the leaky drinking-trough under the elm tree
where the horses used to stand.

Then came night
that was like falling water.
At times, for hours,
a bird spirit,
half buzzard, half swan,
just above the rushes
from which a snow-storm howls.

DER SCHLAMMFANG

Eines Abends kamen
aus einem Loch im Asphalt
Männer mit Masken.
Sie rochen nach seifigem Schlamm,
im Netzwerk trug einer
tote Fische
und grüne Wasserratten.
Abwässer liefen von ihren Stiefeln.
Niemand wollte sie sehen
in der Stadt,
jeder schloss die Tür.
Sie zogen über den Markt und schwanden
im Gebüsch verkohlter Schrebergärten.
Eine schillernde Muschel
hing einem im Haar.
Noch lange glomm sie
im öligen Spiegel der Strasse.

THE MUDCATCHERS

One night from a hole in the asphalt
masked men arrived.
They smelled of soapy mud.
In his net
one of them carried
dead fish
and green water rats.
Effluent oozed from their boots.
No one wanted to see them
in the town,
everyone locked his door.
They crossed the market square and vanished
in the shrubs of the small allotments.
A glittering mussel shell
clung to the hair of one.
For a long time it glimmered
in the street's oily mirror.

MIDDLEHAM CASTLE

Vertraut mit den Gewohnheiten grosser Wälder,
das Jahr streift in den Farben des Eichelhähers
die schmerzliche Helle erstarrter Äste,
das Winterhaar des Hirsches klebt an der Rinde,
die Kälber stehen abends dicht gedrängt,
sich wärmend an der Wolke des eigenen Atems,
zieh ich mit Stricken und Pferden die Stämme
den Ginsterhügel hinauf nach Middleham Castle.

Dies will ich bezeugen, beim Herdfeuer hier.
Im Mond sah ich den hinkenden Schatten
des Königs, Gloster ging um, in Rot gekleidet,
den schmutzigen Zobel über dem Buckel,
das kurze Schwert am Gürtel. Er kroch
durch mächtige Wurzeln der Eiche in die Erde.
Dort lag ein Klumpen geronnenen Bluts,
aus dem er Ketten und Ringe zerrte.

In Nächten langer Helle
steht er im brüchigen Schatten
des Faulbaums an der Mauer,
die weissen Schwalben
nisten in seinem Zimmer.

Er stieg aus seiner Grube,
gräserstill,
die Wolfsmilch ätzte seine Spur.
Hornissen schwärmten,
der Überfall von Blüten
konnt ihn nicht ersticken.

Wurmstichig ist sein Fuss.
Die Steine schleifend,
geht Gloster zu den Ställen.
Die Doggen senken ihren Kopf
dem Peitschenhieb entgegen.

MIDDLEHAM CASTLE

Familiar with the ways of great forests—
the year streaks with the colour of jays
the painful brightness of branches grown rigid,
the stag's winter hairs stick to the bark,
when light begins to fall the fawns huddle,
warming themselves on the cloud of their own breath—
with ropes and horses I haul the tree-trunks
up the gorse hill to Middleham Castle.

So much let me set down, here by the stove's fire.
In the moon I saw the limping shadow
of the King, Gloucester wandered about, dressed in red,
a dirty sable slung over his hump,
a dagger in his belt. He crept
into earth, through the great roots of an oak.
There lay a lump of congealed blood
from which he pulled chains and rings.

In nights of long brightness
he stands in the broken shadow
of the black alder by the wall,
the white swallows
nest in his room.

He came out of his burrow,
quiet as grass,
spurge ate into his track.
Hornets swarmed,
the assault of blossoms
could not stifle him.

His foot is worm-eaten.
Dragging on stones,
Gloucester walks to the stables.
The mastiffs lower their heads
towards the lash of his whip.

Knechte sind wir
und fürchten sein Messer,
liegt auch sein Schädel,
von vielen Wintern kahlgepickt,
tief in der Erde.

MACBETH

Mit Hexen redete ich,
in welcher Sprache,
ich weiss es nicht mehr.

Aufgesprengt
die Tore des Himmels,
freigelassen der Geist,
in Windwirbeln
das Gelichter der Heide.

Am Meer
die schmutzigen Zehen des Schnees,
hier wartet einer
mit Händen ohne Haut.
Ich wollt, meine Mutter
hätt mich erstickt.

Aus den Ställen des Winds
wird er kommen,
wo die alten Frauen
das Futter häckseln.

Argwohn mein Helm,
ich häng ihn
ins Gebälk der Nacht.

We are slaves
and fear his knife,
though his head,
picked bare by many winters,
lies deep in the earth.

MACBETH

I talked with witches,
in what language,
I don't remember.

Blasted open
the gates of Heaven,
the spirit unleashed,
in whirlwinds
the heath folk.

By the sea
the dirty toes of the snow,
here waits a man
with skinless hands.
I wish my mother
had suffocated me.

From the stables of the wind
he will come,
where the old women
chop up chaff for fodder.

Suspicion, my helmet,
I'll hang it up
on the rafters of night.

DIE NACHBARN

Für Hermann Kesten

Die Ruhe des Stroms,
das Feuer der Erde,
die leere Finsternis des Himmels
sind meine gefährlichen Nachbarn.

Der Reiher kann sich von vielen Seen
das seichte schilfige Wasser wählen,
wo er mit jähem Stoss
die Beute greift und tötet.

Nicht kann das Wasser
den Reiher wählen.
Geduldig trägt es die Furcht der Fische,
den heiseren Schrei des hungrigen Vogels.

Wasser und Reiher,
beide sind Nachbarn
von hohen Erlen,
von Rohr und Fröschen.

Geknetet in Gleichmut,
essen die Menschen, meine Nachbarn,
täglich ihr Brot.
Keiner will Asche sein.

Keinem gelingt es,
die Münze zu prägen,
die noch gilt
in eisiger Nacht.

MY NEIGHBOURS

for Hermann Kesten

The river's calm,
the fire of earth,
the sky's empty darkness
are my dangerous neighbours.

The heron can choose among many lakes
the shallow rushy water
where with a sudden thrust
he seizes his prey and kills it.

But water cannot
choose its heron.
Patiently it endures the fishes' fear,
the hoarse cry of the hungry bird.

Water and heron,
both are neighbours
of tall alders,
of reeds and frogs.

Kneaded in equanimity,
human beings, my neighbours,
eat their daily bread.
None wants to be ashes.

None succeeds
in minting the coin
that remains valid
in an icy night.

DIE ENGEL

Ein Rauch,
ein Schatten steht auf,
geht durch das Zimmer,
wo eine Greisin,
den Gänseflügel
in schwacher Hand,
den Sims des Ofens fegt.
Ein Feuer brennt.
Gedenke meiner,
flüstert der Staub.

Novembernebel, Regen, Regen
und Katzenschlaf.
Der Himmel schwarz
und schlammig über dem Fluss.
Aus klaffender Leere fliesst die Zeit,
fliesst über die Flossen
und Kiemen der Fische
und über die eisigen Augen
der Engel,
die niederfahren hinter der dünnen Dämmerung,
mit russigen Schwingen zu den Töchtern Kains.

Ein Rauch,
ein Schatten steht auf,
geht durch das Zimmer.
Ein Feuer brennt.
Gedenke meiner,
flüstert der Staub.

THE ANGELS

A wisp of smoke,
a shadow rises
crosses the room
where an old woman,
a goose's wing
in her feeble hand,
sweeps the stove ledge.
A fire is burning.
Remember me,
whispers the dust.

November mist, rain, rain
and the sleep of cats.
The sky black
and miry above the river.
From gaping emptiness time flows,
flows over the fins
and gills of fish
and over the icy eyes
of the angels
who descend behind the thin dusk,
with sooty wings to the daughters of Cain.

A wisp of smoke,
a shadow rises,
crosses the room.
A fire is burning.
Remember me,
whispers the dust.

UNTER DER BLANKEN HACKE DES MONDS
werde ich sterben,
ohne das Alphabet der Blitze
gelernt zu haben.

Im Wasserzeichen der Nacht
die Kindheit der Mythen,
nicht zu entziffern.

Unwissend
stürz ich hinab,
zu den Knochen der Füchse geworfen.

GEHÖLZ, *Für Heinrich Böll*
habichtsgrau,
das Grillenlicht der Mittagsdürre,
dahinter das Haus,
gebaut auf eine Wasserader.

Wasser,
verborgen,
in sandiger Öde,
du strömtest in den Durst der Sprache,
du zogst die Blitze an.

Am Eingang der Erde,
sagt eine Stimme, wo Steine
und Wurzeln die Tür verriegeln,
sind die zerwühlten Knochen Hiobs
zu Sand geworden, dort steht noch
sein Napf voll Regenwasser.

UNDER THE MOON'S BRIGHT MATTOCK
I shall die,
without having learnt
lightning's alphabet.

In night's watermark
the childhood of myths,
indecipherable.

Ignorant
I plunge down,
flung to the bones of foxes.

SPINNEY, *for Heinrich Böll*
hawk-grey,
the cricket light of noon dryness,
behind them, the house,
built on a vein of water.

Water,
hidden,
in sandy wilderness,
you flowed into the thirst of language,
you attracted lightning.

At the entrance to earth,
says a voice, where stones
and roots bolt the door,
the grubbed-up bones of Job
have turned to sand, there still
his bowl of rain water stands.

APRIL '63

Aufblickend vom Hauklotz
im leichten Regen,
das Beil in der Hand,
seh ich dort oben im breiten Geäst
fünf junge Eichelhäher.

Sie jagen lautlos, geben Zeichen
von Ast zu Ast,
sie weisen der Sonne
den Weg durchs Nebelgebüsch.
Und eine feurige Zunge fährt in die Bäume.

Ich bette mich ein
in die eisige Mulde meiner Jahre.
Ich spalte Holz,
das zähe splittrige Holz der Einsamkeit.
Und siedle mich an
im Netz der Spinnen,
die noch die Öde des Schuppens vermehren,
im Kiengeruch
gestapelter Zacken,
das Beil in der Hand.

Aufblickend vom Hauklotz
im warmen Regen des April,
seh ich an blanken
Kastanienästen
die leimigen Hüllen
der Knospen glänzen.

APRIL '63

Eyes raised from the chopping block
in light rain,
holding the axe,
up there in the wide branches
I see five young jays.

In silence they hunt, signal
from bough to bough,
show sunrays the way
through hazy scrub.
And a fiery tongue strikes the trees.

I bed down
in the icy hollow of my years.
I split wood,
the tough splintery wood of loneliness.
And settle into
the spiders' webs
that deepen the shed's desolation,
in the pine resin odour
of twigs piled up,
holding the axe.

Eyes raised from the chopping block
in warm April rain,
on bare
chestnut boughs
I see the gluey husks
of the buds gleam.

MEINUNGEN

Die Leute sagen im Ort:
Drei Kieselsteine,
vor eine Strassenwalze
geworfen.

Die Freunde sagen:
Tauwetter kommt
und legen beschneite Mäntel ab.

Einer, für Jahre
eingesessen in Bautzen,
stellt sich ans Fenster und liest.

Bald füllt sich das Zimmer
mit jungen und alten Stimmen,
mit Tabak und Asche,
mit Hoffnung und Zweifel.

Die Katzen,
die hinter der Tür
auf der Treppe dämmern,
sind weise und schweigen.

OPINIONS

The local people say:
Three pebbles
thrown in front
of a steamroller.

My friends say:
The thaw is coming
and take off their snow-covered coats.

One who spent years
in the Bautzen camp
goes to the window and reads.

Soon the room fills
with young and old voices,
with tobacco and ash,
with hope and doubt.

The cats, dozing
behind the door
on the landing, in halflight,
are wise and keep silent.

PE-LO-THIEN

Lass mich bleiben
im weissen Gehölz,
Verwalter des Windes
und der Wolken. Erhell
die Gedanken einsamer Felsen.

Aus eisigen Wassern
tauchen die Tage auf,
störrisch und blind.
Mit geschundenen Masken
suchen sie frierend
das dünne Reisigfeuer
des Verfemten,
der hinter der Mauer lebt
mit seinen Kranichen und Katzen.

PE-LO-TIEN*

Let me stay
in the white wood,
caretaker of the wind
and the clouds. Brighten
the thoughts of lonely rocks.

From icy waters
the days emerge,
stubborn and blind.
With ravaged masks
freezing they look for
the thin brushwood fire
of the outlawed man
who lives behind the wall
with his cranes and cats.

---

*Also known as Po-Chü-I (A.D. 772-846)

AM TAGE MEINES FORTGEHNS
entweichen die Dohlen
durchs glitzernde Netz der Mücken.

Am Acker klebt
der Rauch des Güterzuges,
der Himmel regenzwirnig,
dann grau gewalkt,
ein schweres Tuch,
niedergezogen
von der nassen Fahrspur.

Namen,
vernarbt und überwuchert
von neuen Zellen,
wie die verzerrte Schrift
im Baum —
ein eisiger Hauch
fegt über die Tenne der Worte.
Die Mittagsdistel erlosch
im heuigen Licht der Scheune.

Die leichte Dünung
wehender Gräser
verebbt an den Steinen.
Gealtert
geht das Jahr
mit stumpfer Axt, ein Tagelöhner,
auf den Spuren des Dachses
über die Hügel davon.
Die Leere saust
in den lehmigen Löchern
der Uferschwalben.

THIS DAY OF MY GOING
the jackdaws veer off
through a glittering net of midges.

To the ploughed field
smoke from the goods train sticks,
the sky threaded with rain,
then greyly fulled,
a heavy cloth
pulled down
by the wet wheel track.

Names,
cicatrised, overgrown
by new cells
like the distorted letters
in the tree's bark —
an icy breath
sweeps the threshing-floor of words.
The noon thistle went out
in the barn's hay light.

The faint billowing
of wind-blown grasses
ebbs against boulders.
Aged,
the year, a casual labourer,
with a blunt axe follows
the badger's track
over the hills, and away.
In the sand-martins'
loamy nest holes
emptiness roars.

HUBERTUSWEG

Märzmitternacht, sagte der Gärtner,
wir kamen vom Bahnhof
und sahen das Schlusslicht des späten Zuges
im Nebel erlöschen. Einer ging hinter uns,
wir sprachen vom Wetter.
Der Wind wirft Regen
aufs Eis der Teiche,
langsam dreht sich das Jahr ins Licht.

Und in der Nacht
das Sausen in den Schlüssellöchern.
Die Wut des Halms
zerreisst die Erde.
Und gegen Morgen wühlt
das Licht das Dunkel auf.
Die Kiefern harken Nebel von den Fenstern.

Dort unten steht,
armselig wie abgestandener Tabakrauch,
mein Nachbar, mein Schatten
auf der Spur meiner Füsse, verlass ich das Haus.
Missmutig gähnend
im stäubenden Regen der kahlen Bäume
bastelt er heute am rostigen Maschendraht.
Was fällt für ihn ab, schreibt er die Fahndung
ins blaue Oktavheft, die Autonummern meiner Freunde,
die leicht verwundbare Strasse belauernd,
die Konterbande,
verbotene Bücher,
Brosamen für die Eingeweide,
versteckt im Mantelfutter.
Ein schwaches Feuer nähre mit einem Ast.

Ich bin nicht gekommen,
das Dunkel aufzuwühlen.
Nicht streuen will ich vor die Schwelle
die Asche meiner Verse,
den Eintritt böser Geister zu bannen.

THE STREET

March midnight, the gardener said,
on our way from the station,
as we saw the rear light of a late train
fade out in the fog. Somebody walked behind us,
we talked of the weather.
The wind hurls rain
on to the ice of the ponds,
slowly the year is turning into the light.

And all that night
a roar in the keyholes.
The grassblade's fury
lashes the earth.
And around daybreak light
churns up the dark.
The pines rake fog from the window-panes.

Down there, wretched
as tobacco smoke left behind,
stands my neighbour, the shadow
that trails my feet, if I leave the house.
Glumly yawning
in the bare trees' drizzle
today he's tinkering with rusty wire on the fence.
What's it worth to him, if he notes the accusing facts
in his blue exercise book, the car numbers of my friends,
keeps an eye on a street so vulnerable,
on the contraband,
forbidden books,
crumbs for our stomachs,
concealed in coat linings.
A single twig thrown on a feeble fire.

I have not come
to churn up the dark.
Nor will I scatter in front of my threshold
the ash of my verses
to keep evil spirits out.

An diesem Morgen
mit nassem Nebel
auf sächsisch-preussischer Montur,
verlöschenden Lampen an der Grenze,
der Staat die Hacke,
das Volk die Distel,
steig ich wie immer
die altersschwache Treppe hinunter.

Vor der Keilschrift von Ras Schamra
seh ich im Zimmer meinen Sohn
den ugaritischen Text entziffern,
die Umklammerung
von Traum und Leben,
den friedlichen Feldzug des Königs Keret.
Am siebenten Tag,
wie IL der Gott verkündet,
kam heisse Luft und trank die Brunnen aus,
die Hunde heulten,
die Esel schrieen laut vor Durst.
Und ohne Sturmbock ergab sich eine Stadt.

This morning
with damp fog
on its Prussian-Saxon uniform,
with fading lights on the frontier,
the State a mattock,
the people a thistle,
I descend as usual
the decrepit stairs.

In the room I see my son
decipher the Ugaritic text
of Ras Shamra's cuneiform,
the bracketing
of dream and life,
the peaceable campaign of King Keret.
On the seventh day
as IL the god proclaims,
came hot air to drink dry the wells,
the dogs howled,
the donkeys cried out with thirst.
And no battering ram was needed to make a city surrender.

UNKRAUT

Auch jetzt, wo der Putz sich beult
und von der Mauer des Hauses blättert,
die Metastasen des Mörtels
in breiten Strängen sichtbar werden,
will ich mit blossem Finger
nicht schreiben in die porige Wand
die Namen meiner Feinde.

Der rieselnde Schutt ernährt das Unkraut,
Brennesseln, kalkig blass,
wuchern am rissigen Rand der Terrasse.
Die Kohlenträger, die mich abends
heimlich mit Koks versorgen,
die Körbe schleppen zur Kellerschütte,
sind unachtsam, sie treten
die Nachtkerzen nieder.
Ich richte sie wieder auf.

Willkommen sind Gäste,
die Unkraut lieben,
die nicht scheuen den Steinpfad,
vom Gras überwachsen.
Es kommen keine.

Es kommen Kohlenträger,
sie schütten aus schmutzigen Körben
die schwarze kantige Trauer
der Erde in meinen Keller.

WEEDS

Even now that the paintwork blisters
and flakes from the walls of my house,
the metastases of mortar
reveal themselves in wide streaks,
with my bare finger I will not
inscribe on the porous wall
the names of my enemies.

By trickling soot the weeds
are nourished, nettles, chalky-white,
grow rank in the cracks of the terrace.
And coalmen who at night
in secret provide me with coke,
dragging their baskets to the cellar chute,
are careless, they stamp
my evening primroses down.
I raise them up again.

I welcome guests
who are fond of weeds,
who do not avoid the paved
path overgrown with grass.
They do not come.

It is the coalmen who come,
to pour from grimy baskets
the black sharp-edged sadness
of earth into my cellar.

DAS GERICHT

Nicht dafür geboren,
unter den Fittichen der Gewalt zu leben,
nahm ich die Unschuld des Schuldigen an.

Gerechtfertigt
durch das Recht der Stärke,
sass der Richter an seinem Tisch,
unwirsch blätternd in meinen Akten.

Nicht gewillt,
um Milde zu bitten,
stand ich vor den Schranken,
in der Maske des untergehenden Monds.

Wandanstarrend
sah ich den Reiter, ein dunkler Wind
verband ihm die Augen,
die Sporen der Disteln klirrten.
Er hetzte unter Erlen den Fluss hinauf.

Nicht jeder geht aufrecht
durch die Furt der Zeiten.
Vielen reisst das Wasser
die Steine unter den Füssen fort.

Wandanstarrend,
nicht fähig,
den blutigen Dunst
noch Morgenröte zu nennen,
hörte ich den Richter
das Urteil sprechen,
zerbrochene Sätze aus vergilbten Papieren.
Er schlug den Aktendeckel zu.

Unergründlich,
was sein Gesicht bewegte.
Ich blickte ihn an
und sah seine Ohnmacht.
Die Kälte schnitt in meine Zähne.

THE LAW COURT

Not born
to live under the wings of despotism
I assumed the innocence of the guilty man.

Justified
by the right of power
the judge sat at his table
testily turning the leaves of my file.

Not prepared
to beg for mercy
I stood at the bar
in the mask of the setting moon.

Staring at the wall
I saw the horseman, a dark wind
blindfolding him,
the spurs of the thistles clanged.
Under alders he galloped up-river.

Not every one walks upright
through the ford of the ages.
For many the current pulls
pebbles from under their feet.

Staring at the wall,
not able
to call that bloody haze
by its old name of sunrise,
I heard the judge
pronounce his verdict,
broken phrases from yellowed papers.
He slapped the folder shut.

Unfathomable—
that which moved his features.
I looked at him
and saw his impotence.
The cold cut into my teeth.

DIE NEUNTE STUNDE
(1979)

DER HOLUNDER öffnet die Monde,
alles geht ins Schweigen hinüber,
die fliessenden Lichter im Bach,
das durch Wasser getriebene
Planetarium des Archimedes,
astronomische Zeichen,
in den Anfängen babylonisch.

Sohn,
kleiner Sohn Enkidu,
du verliessest deine Mutter, die Gazelle,
deinen Vater, den Wildesel,
um mit der Hure nach Uruk zu gehen.
Die milchtragenden Ziegen flohen.
Es verdorrte die Steppe.

Hinter dem Stadttor
mit den sieben Eisenriegeln
unterwies dich Gilgamesch,
der Grenzgänger zwischen Himmel und Erde,
die Stricke des Todes zu durchhauen.

Finster brannte der Mittag auf dem Ziegelwerk,
finster lag das Gold in der Kammer des Königs.
Kehre um, Enkidu.
Was schenkte dir Gilgamesch?
Das schöne Haupt der Gazelle versank.
Der Staub schlug deine Knochen.

THE ELDER TREE opens its moons,
all passes into silence,
the flowing lights in the stream,
the planetarium of Archimedes
driven through water,
astronomical signs
that came from Babylon.

Son,
little son Enkidu,
you left your mother, the gazelle,
your father, the wild donkey,
to go with the whore to Uruk.
The milk-bearing goats fled.
The steppe withered.

Behind the city gate
with its seven iron bolts
you were instructed by Gilgamesh,
who crosses the frontier between heaven and earth,
to slash the ropes of death.

Darkly noon burned on the brickworks,
darkly the gold lay in the king's room.
Turn back, Enkidu.
What did Gilgamesh give you?
The gazelle's lovely head submerged.
Dust beat your bones.

DER AMMONITER

Überdrüssig der Götter und ihrer Feuer
lebte ich ohne Gesetz
in der Senke des Tales Hinnom.
Mich verliessen die alten Begleiter,
das Gleichgewicht von Erde und Himmel,
nur der Widder, die Moderhinke
schleifend über die Sterne, blieb mir treu.
Unter seinem Gehörn aus Stein,
das rauchlos glänzte, schlief ich nachts,
brannte Urnen jeden Tag,
die ich abends vor der Sonne
am Felsen zerschlug.
Nicht sah ich in den Zedern
die Katzendämmerung, den Aufflug des Vogels,
die Herrlichkeit des Wassers,
das über meine Arme rann,
wenn ich im Bottich schlämmte den Ton.
Der Geruch des Todes machte mich blind.

THE AMMONITE

Tired of the gods and of their fires,
I lived without laws
in the dip of the valley of Hinnom.
My old companions left me,
the balance of earth and sky,
only the ram, trailing its footrot limp
across the stars, remained loyal.
Under its horns of stone
that shone without smoke, I slept by night,
every day baked urns
that I shattered against the rock
in face of the setting sun.
In the cedars I did not see
the cats' twilight, the rising of birds,
the splendour of water
flowing over my arms
when in my bucket I mixed clay.
The smell of death made me blind.

MELPOMENE

Bitterstachlig der Wald,
kein Küstenwind, kein Vorgebirge,
Das Gras verfilzt, der Tod wird kommen
mit Pferdehufen, endlos
über die Steppenhügel, wir gingen zurück,
am Himmel suchend das Kastell,
das nicht zu schleifen war.

Feindselig die Dörfer,
die Hütten hastig geräumt,
im Dachgebälk geräucherte Haut,
Fangnetze und Knochenamulette.
Überall im Land nur böse Verehrung,
Tierhäupter im Nebel, Wahrsagerei
aus geschnittenen Weidenruten.

Später, im Norden,
hirschäugige Männer
jagten auf Pferden vorbei.
Wir begruben die Toten.
Mühsam war es,
die Axt ins Erdreich zu schlagen,
Feuer musste den Boden auftauen.

Das Blut geopferter Hähne
wurde nicht angenommen.

MELPOMENE

The forest bitter, spiky,
no shore breeze, no foothills,
the grass grows matted, death will come
with horses' hooves, endlessly
over the steppes' mounds, we went back,
searching the sky for the fort
that could not be razed.

The villages hostile,
the cottages cleared out in haste,
smoked skin on the attic beams,
snare netting, bone amulets.
All over the country an evil reverence,
animals' heads in the mist, divination
by willow wands.

Later, up in the North,
stag-eyed men
rushed by on horseback.
We buried the dead.
It was hard
to break the soil with our axes,
fire had to thaw it out.

The blood of sacrificed cockerels
was not accepted.

DAS GRAB DES ODYSSEUS

Niemand wird finden
das Grab des Odysseus,
kein Spatenstich
den krustigen Helm
im Dunst versteinerter Knochen.

Such nicht die Höhle,
wo unter die Erde hinab
ein wehender Russ, ein Schatten nur,
vom Pech der Fackel versehrt,
zu seinen toten Gefährten ging,
die Hände hebend waffenlos,
bespritzt mit dem Blut geschlachteter Schafe.

Mein ist alles, sagte der Staub,
das Grab der Sonne hinter der Wüste,
die Riffe voller Wassergetöse,
der endlose Mittag, der immer noch warnt
den Seeräubersohn aus Ithaka,
das Steuerruder, schartig vom Salz,
die Karten und Schiffskataloge
des alten Homer.

THE GRAVE OF ODYSSEUS

No one will find
the grave of Odysseus,
no stab of a spade
the encrusted helmet
in the haze of petrified bones.

Do not look for the cave
where down below the earth
a wafting soot, a mere shadow,
damaged by pitch from torches,
went to its dead companions,
raising weaponless hands,
splattered with blood of slaughtered sheep.

All is mine, said the dust,
the sun's grave behind the desert,
the reefs full of the sea's roar,
unending noon that still warns
the pirate's boy from Ithaca,
the rudder jagged with salt,
the maritime charts and lists
of ancient Homer.

PFEILSPITZE DES ADA

Bewohner der kahlen Berge,
Nachzügler, Zelte, flatternd und finster,
unduldsam der Tod,
als stürze er von der Sonne hinab
in gleissende Ziegelscherben.

Sandkauend, in Stössen
und Wirbeln der Wind,
der heiss durch die Disteln fegt.
Eselfarben die Mauer,
lehmrissig,
der Mann, der sich nähert,
geht ohne Schatten.

Einst fliege ich auf
zu den Gazellen des Lichts,
sagt eine Stimme.

ADA'S ARROWHEAD

Inhabitants of the bare mountains,
stragglers, tents, flapping and gloomy,
death intolerant
as though it came hurtling down from the sun
into gleaming brick shards.

Chewing sand, in bursts
and whirls the wind
that sweeps hot through thistles.
The walls donkey-coloured,
with cracks in the clay,
the man approaching
walks without a shadow.

One day I shall fly up
to the gazelles of light,
says a voice.

ARISTEAS I

Die erste Frühe,
als im Gewölk das Gold
der Toten lag. Es schlief der Wind,
wo im Geäst
die nebelgefiederte Krähe sass.

Der Vogel flog,
sein Fittich schlug das Licht
im Erlengrau,
die milchige Haut der Steppe.

Ich, Aristeas,
als Krähe einem Gott gefolgt,
ich schweife,
vom Traum gerissen,
durch Lorbeerhaine des Nebels,
mit starrem Flügel den Morgen suchend.
Ich spähte
in schneeverkrustete Höhlen,
Gesichter, einäugig, feuerbeschienen,
versanken im Rauch.
Und Pferde standen, vereist die Mähnen,
an Pflöcke gefesselt mit Riemen aus Russ.

Die Krähe strich
ins winterliche Tor,
strich durch verhungertes Gesträuch.
Frost stäubte auf.
Und eine dürre Zunge sprach:
Hier ist das Vergangene ohne Schmerz.

ARISTEAS I

First glimmer,
when in the clouds lay
the gold of the dead. The wind slept
where deep in branches
sat the fog-plumaged crow.

The bird flew,
its wing beat the light
in the alders' greyness,
the steppe's milky pelt.

    I, Aristeas,
    in crow's guise follower of a god,
    roam far afield,
    swept on by a dream,
    through laurel groves of mist,
    and with stiff wings look out for morning.
    I pried
    into snow-encrusting caverns:
    faces, one-eyed, firelit,
    vanished in smoke.
    And horses, their manes icy,
    tied to posts, waited, with bridles of soot.

The crow passed
through the wintry gate,
passed through starved bushes.
Frost rose like dust.
And a dry tongue uttered:
Here the past gives no pain.

ARISTEAS II

Die Einsamkeit
der Pfähle im brackigen Wasser,
an lecker Bootswand
kratzt eine tote Ratte.
Hier sitze ich mittags,
ein alter Mann,
im Schatten des Hafenschuppens
auf einem Mühlstein.

Flusslotse einst,
doch später fuhr ich Schiffe, arme Frachten,
hoch in den Norden durch die Gezeiten.
Die Kapitäne zahlten mit Konterbande,
es liess sich leben, Weiber genug
und Segeltuch.

Die Namen verdämmern,
keiner entziffert den Text,
der hinter meinen Augen steht.
Ich, Aristeas, Sohn des Kaystrobios,
blieb verschollen,
der Gott verbannte mich
in diesen engen schmutzigen Hafen,
wo unweit der kimmerischen Fähre
das Volk mit Fellen und Amuletten handelt.

Noch stampft die Walkmühle nachts.
Manchmal hocke ich als Krähe
dort oben in der Pappel am Fluss,
reglos in der untergehenden Sonne,
den Tod erwartend,
der auf vereisten Flössen wohnt.

ARISTEAS II

The loneliness
of posts in the brackish water,
at the leaking boards of a boat
a dead rat scratches.
Here I sit at noon,
an old man,
in the harbour shed's shade
on a millstone.

Once a river-barge pilot,
but later I sailed ships, poor cargoes,
high up into the north through the tides.
Captains paid me in contraband,
it was a good life, women enough
and sailcloth.

The names blur,
no one can decipher the text
inscribed behind my eyelids.
I, Aristeas, son of Kaystrobios,
went missing,
the god exiled me
to this narrow, dirty harbour,
where not far from the Kimmerian ferry
people trade in skins and amulets.

Still the fulling mill thumps at night.
Sometimes I crouch as a crow
up there in the riverside poplar,
motionless in the setting sun,
waiting for death
that inhabits iced-up rafts.

BEGEGNUNG

für Michael Hamburger

Schleiereule,
Tochter des Schnees,
dem Nachtwind unterworfen,

doch Wurzeln fassend
mit den Krallen
im modrig grindigen Gemäuer,

Schnabelgesicht
mit runden Augen,
herzstarre Maske
aus Federn weissen Feuers,
das weder Zeit noch Raum berührt,

kalt weht die Nacht
ans alte Gehöft,
im Vorhof fahles Gelichter,
Schlitten, Gepäck, verschneite Laternen,

in den Töpfen Tod,
in den Krügen Gift,
das Testament an den Balken genagelt.

Das Verborgene unter
den Klauen der Felsen,
die Öffnung in die Nacht,
die Todesangst
wie stechendes Salz ins Fleisch gelegt.

Lasst uns niederfahren
in der Sprache der Engel
zu den zerbrochenen Ziegeln Babels.

MEETING

for Michael Hamburger

Barn owl,
daughter of snow,
subject to the night wind,

yet taking root
with her talons
in the rotten scab of walls,

beak face
with round eyes,
heart-rigid mask
of feathers that are a white fire
touching neither time nor space,

coldly the night blows
at the old homestead,
in its yard pale folk,
sledges, baggage, lamps covered with snow,

in the pots death,
in the pitchers poison,
the last will nailed to a post.

The hidden thing
under the rocks' claws,
the opening into night,
terror of death
thrust into flesh like stinging salt.

Let us go down
in the language of angels
to the broken bricks of Babel.

WINTERMORGEN IN IRLAND

Der Teufel sitzt nachts
im Beichtstuhl des Nebels
und spricht die Verzweifelten an.
Am Morgen verwandelt er sich
in eine Elster,
die lautlos über den Hohlweg fliegt.

Im Winterverlies
das brüchige Gold der Toten
am Eichengesträuch.
Licht rodet die Kälte.
Die vertrauten Gesichter der Dächer
erscheinen wieder.

Die Exerzitien
des Windes über dem Meer,
der erste Eselschrei.
Der Schatten eines Vogels schwebt
am hängenden Felsen die Klippe hinauf.

Die Brandung,
der gleitende Wall aus Wasser und Licht,
die irische See
verrät nicht, ob Regen
den Mittag begraben wird.

WINTER MORNING IN IRELAND

At night the devil sits
in the fog's confessional box
and speaks to those in despair.
In the morning he turns
into a magpie
that flies off over the gorge without a sound.

In winter's dungeon
the brittle gold of the dead
on the oak scrub.
Light thins out the cold.
The familiar faces of roofs
reappear.

The spiritual exercises
of the wind over the sea,
the first donkey cry.
A bird's shadow hovers
up the cliff over hanging rock.

The surf,
the sliding wall of water and light,
the Irish Sea
does not divulge whether rain
will bury noon.

JAN-FELIX CAERDAL

für Günter Eich

Am Ende der Öde
sah ich die grosse Eskorte,
das Banner zerfetzt, die Trommel durchlöchert,
die Sänfte,
von acht zerlumpten Knechten getragen,
war leer.

Einem Toten,
die Arme zerbrachen wie trockene Äste,
gelang im Sturz der Stirnaufschlag.

Ich, der Bretone,
mit meerdurchsickerten Schuhen
und einem Hemd aus Nebel
über dem Sonnengeflecht,

ich, der Nachzügler,
der einst
Geschmeide wie Ähren auflas,
im Licht der Messe versank,

ging nun voran
mit leeren Händen
und einer Rinne Salz im Gesicht.

JAN-FELIX CAERDAL

for Günter Eich

At the waste land's edge
I saw the great convoy,
their banner torn, their drum pierced,
the litter,
carried by eight servants in rags,
was empty.

A dead man,
his arms snapped like dry sticks,
succeeded in touching the ground with his brow as he fell.

I, the Breton,
my shoes soaked in sea water,
in a shirt of fog over my diaphragm,

I, the straggler
who once
gathered up jewels like ears of corn,
sank in the light of the Mass,

now walked in the van
with empty hands
and a furrow of salt in my face.

IN MEMORIAM GÜNTER EICH

Hinfliessen wird der Himmel,
aber wir werden dem Schnee,
der ins schwarze Wasser sinkt,
kein Tedeum mehr sprechen.

Ein verwüstetes Haus zwischen Himmel und Erde.
Im Torweg die Kröte,
noch immer
die goldene Krone auf dem Kopf.

PHILIPP

Hier endet der Weg,
die Fangschnur hängt
vereist
im Erlengestrüpp.

Die grashaarigen Kinder
verleugnen das Licht
und suchen den Schnee,
der mit den Krähen über die Berge kommt.

Die schweigsamen Kinder
am Eingang der Nacht,
Wind wickelt sie ein ins kühle Tuch,
das nicht den Abdruck der Erde zeigt.

IN MEMORIAM GÜNTER EICH

The sky will drift away,
but we shall speak no Te Deum
for the snow
that goes down in black water.

A ravaged house between sky and earth.
In its gateway, the toad,
even now
with the golden crown on its head.

PHILIP

Here the way ends,
the snare, iced up,
hangs
in the alder scrub.

The grass-haired children
deny light
and look for the snow
that comes with the crows across the mountains.

The taciturn children
at the entrance to night,
wind wraps them in a cool cloth
that does not show the imprint of earth.

FRIEDE

Zugzeiten der Vögel.
In den stachligen
Grannen gedroschener Ähren
wohnt noch die milde Leere des Sommers.
In den Schiessscharten des Wasserturms
wuchert das Gras.

SCHOTTISCHER SOMMER

    'What seemed corporeal melted as breath into the wind'
                              Shakespeare, *Macbeth*

Schottischer Sommer,
unter der Eiche
zopftrocken
sitzend die Weiber aus Cawdor,
manche verborgen im Licht der Wolken,
abgeblühte Nesseln im Sand.
Über die Felsen herab
Trompetenstösse, ein Klirren
wühlt die Brandung auf.

Nebel, der sie erzeugte,
bald ist es Winter,
dünnes, nie ruhendes Holz,
der Schnee fegt hin und her
und stäubt die Öde an.

Dürr und düster
vor der goldenen Naht des Abends
hocken sie auf zerrissenen Fellen.
Wenn der Mond
die Zeiger verrückt am Turm,
starren sie mit erloschenen Augen.
Unbewohnbar die Trauer,
die an den Klippen verebbt.

PEACE

Migration times of the birds.
In the prickly
awns of thrashed ears of corn
summer's gentle emptiness lingers.
In firing slits of the water tower
grass proliferates.

SCOTTISH SUMMER

> 'What seemed corporeal melted as breath into the wind'
> Shakespeare: *Macbeth*

Scottish summer,
under the oaktree
dry as a plait of hair
sit the women of Cawdor,
some of them hidden in the clouds' light,
nettles, their blossom shed, in the sand.
Down over the rocks
trumpet blasts, a clatter
whips up the sea swell.

Fog that engendered it,
soon it will be winter,
thin wood never at rest,
snow flurries this way and that,
finely dusting the wilderness.

Dried up and dusky
they squat on tattered furs
before evening's golden seam.
When the moon
shifts the clock hands on the tower
they stare with dimmed eyes.
Uninhabitable this grief
that ebbs from the cliffs.

IN BUD

Nachts
das trockene Husten den Flur entlang,
ich öffne die Tür
und atme den Netzgeruch des Alten,
der unter den Klippen blieb.

Die See schreibt
in der Schrift der Algen
die letzte Seite des Logbuchs
auf salzige Felsen—
verleugne die Heimkehr,
sei unterwegs
auf Meeren mit stürzendem Himmelsstrich,
wo jeder Name verlorengeht.

AT BUD

By night
the dry coughing along the corridor.
I open the door
and inhale the net smell of the old man
who was left under the cliffs.

The sea writes
in seaweed script
the last page of the logbook
on to salty rocks—
renounce your homecoming,
be on your way
on oceans with a falling skyline
where every name is lost.

ZNOROVY

für Jan Skácel

Zwischen Kiefer und Brache
die Durchfahrt zum Sommer,
im Gestrüpp, seitwärts, nahe den Scheunen,
die Marderfalle, eingerostet.

Ich werde nie nach Znorovy kommen,
wo die Schatten gefesselt
aus dem Wasser steigen,
der Göpel ohne Pferdegespann
sich lautlos dreht,
das späte Gezeter der Drossel
die Dächer verdunkelt.

Fragwürdig alles,
wenn die Sonne hinter dem Nebel
die Kapsel des Mohns verholzt
und die Körner härter rascheln.
Kein Seismograph
zeigt die Erschütterung der Wesen an.

Was zwingt dich,
nachts an der alten Chaussee zu stehn?
Die mährische Kutsche
mit brüchigem Lederdach
rollt nicht mehr, verfolgt von Buchenblättern,
am grauen Gehöft vorbei.

Der Baummarder liegt im kahlen Geäst
und blickt in die Kühle der Nacht.
Du wartest auf andere Zeichen.

ZNOROVY

for Jan Skácel

Between pine and fallow land
the cart track that leads to summer,
in the scrub, to one side, near the barns
the marten trap, rusted up.

I shall never come to Znorovy
where the shadows rise
fettered out of the waters,
the gin without a team
silently turns,
the late bickering of the thrush
darkens the roofs.

All's questionable
when the sun behind mist
hardens the poppy capsules
and the seedgrains rattle harder.
No seismograph
shows the shaking-up of creatures.

What forces you
to stand by night at the cold road's verge?
The Moravian coach
with its cracked leather roof
no longer rolls, followed by beech leaves,
past the grey homestead.

The pine marten lurks in bare branches
and peers into the coolness of night.
You are waiting for other signs.

DIE NEUNTE STUNDE

Die Hitze sticht in den Stein
das Wort des Propheten.
Ein Mann steigt mühsam
den Hügel hinauf,
in seiner Hirtentasche
die neunte Stunde,
den Nagel und den Hammer.

Der trockene Glanz der Ziegenherde
reisst in der Luft
und fällt als Zunder hinter den Horizont.

BLICK AUS DEM WINTERFENSTER

Kopfweiden, schneeumtanzt,
Besen, die den Nebel fegen.
Holz und Unglück
wachsen über Nacht.
Mein Messgerät
die Fieberkurve.

Wer geht dort ohne Licht
und ohne Mund,
schleift übers Eis
das Tellereisen?

Die Wahrsager des Waldes,
die Füchse mit schlechtem Gebiss
sitzen abseits im Dunkel
und starren ins Feuer.

THE NINTH HOUR

Heat stabs into rock,
the prophet's word.
A man makes his way
up the hill,
in his herdsman's scrip
the ninth hour,
the nail and the hammer.

The dry gleam of the goat flock
splits
and drops as tinder behind the horizon.

VIEW FROM THE WINTER WINDOW

Pollarded willows, the snow dancing round them,
brooms that sweep the mist.
Wood and misfortune
shoot up overnight.
My gauge
is the temperature chart.

Who goes there without a light,
without a mouth,
sliding a steel trap
across the ice?

The soothsayers of the forest,
the foxes with bad teeth
sit in the dark, apart,
staring into the fire.

ÖSTLICHER FLUSS

Such nicht die Steine
im Wasser über dem Schlamm,
der Kahn ist fort,
der Fluss
nicht mehr mit Netzen
und Reusen bestückt.
Der Sonnendocht,
die Sumpfdotterblume verglomm im Regen.

Nur die Weide gibt noch Rechenschaft,
in ihren Wurzeln
sind die Geheimnisse
der Landstreicher verborgen,
die kümmerlichen Schätze,
der rostige Angelhaken,
die Büchse ohne Boden
zum Aufbewahren längst
vergessener Gespräche.

An den Zweigen
die leeren Nester der Beutelmeisen,
die vogelleichten Schuhe.
Keiner streift sie
den Kindern über die Füsse.

EASTERN RIVER

Do not look for the stones
in water above the mud,
the boat is gone.
No longer with nets and baskets
the river is dotted.
The sun wick,
the marsh marigolds flickered out in the rain.

Only the willow bears witness still,
in its roots
the secrets of tramps lie hidden,
their paltry treasures,
the rusty fishhook,
the tin with no bottom
in which to preserve
long-forgotten talks.

On the boughs,
empty nests of the penduline titmice,
shoes light as birds.
No one slips them
over children's feet.

MEIN GROSSVATER

Tellereisen legen,
das Aufspüren des Marders bei frischem Schnee,
das Stellen von Reusen im Mittelgraben,
das war sein Metier.

Für die Auerhahnjagd
die curische Büchse.
Sie schoss ein Blei,
das nicht stärker als ein Kirschkern war.

Er pirschte mit dem Jagdhund voraus,
ich verkroch mich in den blakenden Abend,
sah über der verschneiten Eiche
am Himmel den Hirsch verbluten.

Was wär, wenn ich fortliefe
und liesse ihn mit seinen Netzen,
Remisen und Fallen allein?
Ich ging nicht über die sieben Seen.

In strengen Wintern sassen
die Rebhühner nah bei den Scheunen.
Mit rauher Zunge leckte der Mond
das klamme Fell der Katze.

Scharf und brandig stand die Luft
dort über dem Schnee.
Der Alte kam hinter der Miete hervor
und trug die Flinte ins Haus zurück.

Prophetisch begann die Nacht,
messianisch die erste Stunde.
Er kramte im Bücherkasten und las
die »Volksschriften zur Umwälzung der Geister«.

Er drehte am Messingring der Lampe.
Die Sonne glomm auf,
der Eichelhäher schrie
und flog in den kalten märkischen Morgen.

MY GRANDFATHER

Setting steel traps,
tracking the marten in new snow,
laying creels in the middle ditch,
these were his business.

For the capercailzie shoot
a Courland gun.
It fired a lead pellet
with no more force than a cherrystone.

He roamed on ahead with the hounds,
I crept away into the smoky halflight,
above the snow-laden oaktree saw
the stag bleed to death in the sky.

What if I ran away,
leaving him alone with his nets,
his forest hides and his traps?
I never crossed the seven lakes.

In hard winters the partridges
lay low close to the barns.
Rough-tongued the moon licked
the cat's moist pelt.

Tart and smouldering the air
hung over the snow.
The old man appeared from behind the ricks
and hung up his gun in the house.

Prophetic the night set on,
messianic the first hour.
He searched his bookshelf and read
the 'Popular Writings on the Cataclysm of Spirits'.

He turned the brass screw of the lamp.
The sun glimmered up,
a jay screamed, and flew up
into a cold Brandenburg morning.

DIE KATZE

Der Wintermorgen,
noch dunkel in der Schneeverwehung des Traums,
im Schuppen verstreut
Maiskolbengerippe,
ein Gesicht aus Wasserdunst
vergeht in der Luke.

Was die Katze
hinter den Augen verbirgt,
nicht weiss es der Rauhreif,
das Salz der Hexen.

BRANDENBURG

>>Ach, wie die Nachtviole lieblich duftet!<<
Kleist, *Prinz von Homburg*

Hinter erloschenen Teeröfen
ging ich im Brandgeruch der Kiefernheide,
dort sass ein Knecht am Holzhauerfeuer,
er blickte nicht auf,
er schränkte die Säge.

Noch immer tanzt abends
der rote Ulan
mit Bauerntöchtern auf der Tenne des Nebels,
die Ulanka durchweht
von Mückenschwärmen über dem Moor.

Im Wasserschierling
versunken
die preussische Kalesche.

THE CAT

The winter morning,
dark still in the snowdrift of dream,
scattered round the barn
maize cob skeletons,
a face made of vapour
dissolves in the skylight.

What the cat
hides behind its eyes,
hoarfrost, the salt
of witches, does not know.

BRANDENBURG

> 'Oh, the sweet scent of gilliflowers at night.'
> Kleist: *The Prince of Homburg*

Behind extinguished tar-boiling stoves
I walked in the charry smell of the pine heath,
there a labourer sat by the woodcutters' fire,
he did not look up,
he was setting his saw.

Still in the evenings
the red Uhlan dances
with farmers' daughters on the threshing-floor of the mist,
his tunic exposed to the gust
over the marshes
of swarming gnats.

Gone down into
water hemlock
the Prussian calash.

UNTERWEGS

Die streifende Rotte
vereister Blätter
fällte der Tag
mit Drähten über der Feuergrube.

Neben dem Karren
im Schutz der Plache
die Zigeunerin,
zu ihren Füssen
eingewickelt das schlafende Kind.
Sie hebt aus dem Schafspelz
einen jungen Hund an die Brust,
ihn säugend,
säugt sie den hungrigen Wind im Schnee.

Ferne Tochter
der asiatischen Göttin,
die Feuersteinsichel
hast du verloren
am Rand der höllischen Teiche.
Du hörst das Gebell in der Nacht,
das der Radspur folgt von Lager zu Lager.

ON THE WAY

Day felled
the roaming troop
of ice-covered leaves
with wires above the fire pit.

Beside her wagon,
sheltered by its cover,
the Gipsy woman,
her swaddled infant
asleep at her feet.
From the sheepskin she raises
a puppy to her breast;
suckling it,
she suckles the hungry wind in the snow.

Distant daughter
of the Asiatic goddess,
you've lost your flint sickle
on the edge of the hellish ponds.
In the night you hear the barking
that follows the wheel tracks from camp to camp.

ENTZAUBERUNG

In die Scheunenwand
zeichnet die Nässe
den verfemten König.

Er geht in der Kälte
durchlöcherter Zäune
den lehmigen Feldweg hinunter.
Er zieht am Geschirr
die Maultierstute
mit Körben bepackt, mit Kesseln und Töpfen,
und schwindet im Regen
am Mittelgraben hinter den Weiden.

Es ist Itau,
der Zigeuner, vergangenen Sommer
lag er am Vorwerk im groben Stroh
der rostigen Dreschmaschine.

Die Frau des Pächters erzählt,
sie habe ihn im späten Oktober
am Rand der Brache gesehn.
Er ging im Kreis
und schlug in die Luft das Zeichen,
ein Feuer fuhr aus der Erde,
das ohne Rauch
mit finsterer Flamme versank.

In Wahrheit
zog Itau, der Zigeuner,
im hellen Juli
durchs Bischofslila der Disteln
für immer fort.

THE SPELL BREAKS

On to the barn wall
dampness limns
the outlawed king.

He walks through the chill
of holed fences
down the soft clay of the meadow path.
He tugs at the harness
of his mule jenny
packed with baskets, with kettles and pots
and vanishes in the rain
at the middle ditch behind the willows.

He is Itau
the Gipsy, last summer
he lay by the outwork in the coarse straw
of the rusty threshing machine.

The tenant farmer's wife tells
of seeing him late in October
at the edge of the fallow ground.
He walked in a circle
and into air drew the sign,
a fire rose out of earth,
burned without smoke,
with a dark flame, and subsided.

The truth is
that Itau, the Gipsy,
in bright July
through the thistles' bishop purple,
once and for all, moved on.

BRETONISCHER KLOSTERGARTEN

Der Mittag breitästiger Ulmen.
Der Gichtbrüchige schläft
im Klappstuhl aus Segeltuch.

Engel, schmerzliche Geheimnisse,
gehen durch hohes Gras
und rufen versunkene Namen.

Der leichte Widerhall von Schritten,
Bittgänge, Gespräche im Laub,
nur von der Amsel vernommen.

EIN TOSCANER

Ist es die Stunde,
das Silber von den Dächern zu nehmen,
den Tau von den Blättern des Ölbaums zu schütteln?

Hinfällig
wie der Staub auf vergilbten Manuskripten
ist mein Leben geworden.

Nicht überschreite
die Säulen des Hercules.
Der Tod, der mürrische Maultiertreiber,

ich sah ihn gestern abend am Stall,
umschwirrt von Bremsen,
er weiss den Weg.

Bald deckt
das schwarze Profil der Berge
den Weinstock und die Brunnen zu.

BRETON MONASTERY GARDEN

Noon of wide-branched elms.
The gout-stricken man sleeps
in his canvas folding-chair.

Angels, painful secrets
pass through the high grass
and call out forgotten names.

The faint echo of footfalls,
rogations, talk in the leafage
only the blackbird hears.

A TUSCAN

Is it the hour
to take the silver off the roofs,
to shake the dew off the olive tree's leaves?

Null
as the dust on yellowed manuscripts
my life has become.

Do not pass beyond
the pillars of Hercules.
Death, that surly mule-driver,

last night I saw him near the stable,
horseflies whirring round him,
he knows the way.

Soon
The mountains' black profile
will cover the vine and the wells.

ROM

Vollendeter Sommer,
am äussersten Rand der Sonne
beginnt schon die Finsternis.
Lorbeerverwilderungen,
dahinter aus Disteln und Steinen
ein Versteck,
das sich der Stimme
verweigert.

Transparenz
des Mittagslichtes,
Verse, die an nichts erinnern,
ein helles Wasser
berührt den Mund.

PERSEPHONE

Die Abgründige kam,
stieg aus der Erde,
aufgleissend im Mondlicht.
Sie trug die alte Scherbe im Haar,
die Hüfte an die Nacht gelehnt.

Kein Opferrauch, das Universum
zog in den Duft der Rose ein.

ROME

Replete summer,
at the outermost edge of the sun
already darkness begins.
Laurels gone wild,
behind them a hiding-place
of thistles and stones
that yields
to no voice.

Transparency
of the noon light,
verses that recall nothing,
a bright water
touches the mouth.

PERSEPHONE

The unfathomable came,
rose from the earth,
flaring up in moonlight.
She wore the old shard in her hair,
her hip leaned on night.

No smoke of sacrifice, the universe
entered the fragrance of the rose.

NACHTS

Über den Wolken
das Knarren von Wagenrädern,
Landflüchtige,
unterwegs.

Handfeste Burschen
räumen den Nebel weg,
tragen schlafende Frauen
über die Furt.

Röhricht,
kaum zu erkennen.
Ein Mann,
das Fangnetz über die Schulter geworfen,
steht am Gewässer
und weidet die Fische aus.

Wundmale
die Kiemen der Fische,
sie leuchten im Mond.

Das Wort, ausgesät für die Nacht,
treibt fort, wurzelt im Wind.
Endlos
die Regenlitanei.

BY NIGHT

Above the clouds
the creaking of cartwheels,
fugitives
on their way.

Sturdy fellows
clear away the fog,
carry sleeping women
across the ford.

Rushes,
hardly discernible.
A man,
with a dragnet flung over his shoulders,
stands by the water
and guts the fishes.

Scars
the fishes' gills,
they gleam in moonlight.

The word, sown for the night,
germinates, roots in the wind.
Unending
the litany of the rain.

DIE RÜCKKEHR

Die stumme Gesellschaft,
in Kähnen kam sie hierher,
noch einmal
den ungebrochenen Glanz des Wassers zu sehen,
die Gewissheit des Sommers,
die Hibiscusblüte in der Farbe der Mitra.

Wozu den Sommer beschwören?
Der nubische Steinbock
verliess die Berge,
der Teichrohrsänger flog fort.

Ein Schilfblatt
trieb mit der Strömung vorbei.
Die Kähne versanken
im wässrigen Schatten der Erlen.

THE RETURN

The silent company,
in skiffs it came here
to see once more
the water's unbroken brightness,
the certainty of summer,
the hibiscus flower in the mitre's colour.

Why invoke summer?
The Nubian ilex
left the mountains,
the reed warbler flew off.

A bulrush leaf
drifted by on the current.
The skiffs sank
in the alders' watery shade.

DER KETZER AUS PADUA

I.
Ich kam als Schnee ins Wintergestrüpp
und folgte dem Todeskarren.
Gerechtigkeit und Nachsicht
gab es auf dieser Erde nicht.

Als wollte der lombardische Abend
ein letztes Zeichen setzen,
dort oben, im harschen Astgespinst,
ans Weisse des Himmels
ans Kahle geklammert
die nistende Kälte, das leere Vogelnest.

II.
Und hinter den flachen Kähnen im Kanal
die Stadt der Talare und Horoskope
mit ihren Adepten der Alchimie,
mit feuchten Verliesen
und Folterkammern.

O böser Traum,
da das misshandelte Blut
vom Balken tropfte,
am Eingang der Abtei
das Volk sich duckte
im Stosswind der Schleudermaschine.
Ein Engel stürzte
im rötlichen Dunst der Kirchen und Türme Paduas,
fiel durchs Gestänge
und ruhte mit zerbrochener Schulter
vor einem Horizont aus Hellebarden.
Sein Antlitz erlosch.

III.
Stadt des Marsilius,
das verblakte Pergament
der Propheten
im weissen Feuer des Schnees—

THE HERETIC FROM PADUA

I.
As snow I came into the winter scrub
and followed the death cart.
Justice and understanding
were not to be found on this earth.

As though the Lombard evening
wished to place a last sign,
up there, in the harsh tangle of boughs,
against the white of the sky,
tacked on to the bareness,
the roosting cold, the empty bird's nest.

II.
And behind the flat barges on the canal
the city of scholars' gowns and horoscopes
with its adepts in alchemy,
with damp dungeons
and torture chambers.

O evil dream,
when the maltreated blood
dripped from the beam,
at the abbey's entrance,
the people cringed
in the catapult's blast.
An angel hurtled down
in the reddish vapour of Padua's churches and towers,
crashed through the timbers
and with a broken shoulder came to rest
against a horizon of halberds.
His face extinguished.

III.
City of Marsilius,
the charred parchment
of the prophet
in the snow's white fire—

drei Männer ritten schweigend am Karren vorbei,
Kuriere des Kardinals, da war keine Hufspur,
die zum Frieden führt.

Herr, dein Geheimnis ist gross
und eingeriegelt in die Stille der Felsen,
ich bin nur Staub,
der lockere Ziegel in der Mauer.

   IV.
Die Finsternis kappte die Bäume,
der Schanzkorb versank.
Noch lagen die Toten auf dem Blachfeld.
Das Fussvolk schlug Holz,
der Kalkofen qualmte.

Ich ging ins Gestrüpp, ich schob den Karren,
verurteilt,
den alten Jammer
bis zur Vernichtung der Sinne zu sehen.

three men rode in silence past the cart,
the Cardinal's couriers, there was no hoofprint
leading to peace.

Lord, your secret is great
and bolted into the stillness of rocks,
I am mere dust,
the loose brick in the wall.

   IV.
Darkness polled the trees,
the gabion went down.
Still the dead lay on the fallow field.
The fort soldiers chopped wood,
the limekiln emitted black smoke.

I went into the scrub, I pushed the cart,
condemned
to see the old wretchedness
endure beyond mind's endurance.

NICHTS zu berichten.
Das Einhorn ging fort
und ruht im Gedächtnis der Wälder,

in den Kammern des Mohns,
wenn die Äbtissin Sonne und Mond
den Toten gibt.

Der Herbst lichtet sich,
verliert sein Gedächtnis
in der Blutspur der Buche.

Was bleibt, ist nichts mehr
als der schwarze Draht in der Luft,
der zwei Stimmen vereinigt.

In der weissen Abtei des Winters
ein lautloser Flügelschlag.
Im Namen dessen—
bis ans Ende der Tage.

NOTHING to report.
The unicorn went away
and rests in the wood's memory,

in the poppy's valvules
when the abbess gives sun and moon
to the dead.

Autumn makes a clearing,
loses its memory
in the beech-tree's blood track.

What remains is no more
than the black wire in the air
that connects two voices.

In winter's white abbey
a soundless wingbeat.
In his name who —
to the end of time.

IM KUN-LUN-GEBIRGE

Steig nicht hinauf
ins öde Kun-lun-Gebirge.
Du zahlst an den Pässen
den Geistern Tribut.

Schneemassen verfinstern den Himmel.
Über den Eschen
fliegt ein Falke im Aufwind und schreit.
Er rüttelt und stürzt in die Dunkelheit,
wo die zerspellte Fichte
lautlos im Schnee versinkt.

Vier Tage unterwegs auf steilem Pfad,
der zwischen Felsen und trocknen Tamarisken
sich hochzieht im Kun-lun-Gebirge.

Schneenarben an den Felsen,
Schriftzeichen, nicht zu entziffern.

Und immer die dünne harsche Musik,
die finster das Ohr besetzt.

Und nirgends am Weg die elendste Hütte
aus rohen Fichtenstämmen,
wo man auf nacktem Stroh
sein Haupt betten kann.

Ich irrte umher in schneegreller Nacht
und schlief im grauen Felsenschutt
vor einem Abgrund ein.

In kalter Frühe,
in weisser leuchtender Schneeluft
stieg ich in ein Tal hinab
und folgte der Spur eines Fuchses.

Sie führte zu einem alten Maulbeerbaum
mit einem dünnen Riss in der Rinde.

IN THE KUN-LUN MOUNTAINS

Do not go up
into the desolate Kun-Lun mountains.
At the passes you pay
tribute to the spirits.

Snow masses darken the sky.
Above the ash-trees
a falcon rides the upward airstream and shrieks.
He hovers and plunges into the darkness
where the split fir
sinks in snow without a sound.

Four days' track on the steep path
that rises between rocks and dry tamarisk
in the Kun-Lun mountains.

Snow scars on the rocks,
glyphs, indecipherable.

And always the harsh music
that darkly fills the ear.

And nowhere on that path the most lowly hovel
of raw fir trunks
where on bare straw
one could lay one's head.

I wandered astray in a snow-glaring night
and went to sleep in grey scree
at the edge of a chasm.

In a cold dawn,
in white, shining snow air
I descended to a valley
and followed the trail of a fox.

It led to an ancient mulberry tree
with a narrow cleft in the bark.

Ich öffnete die Rindentür
und stieg in den Baum.
Die Tür fiel raschelnd zu.

Unbeweglich sass ich in der Höhle.
Geister, aus der Materie des wehenden Schnees
besuchten mich nachts
mit Gonggetöse und Trommellärm.

Ich schluckte Wind und Tau
und wagte kaum zu atmen.

Oder sie raunten magische Sprüche,
sie rührten mich an,
ich spürte sie, wir sassen Knie an Knie.
Ich lebte in dunkler Ungewissheit.

Manchmal wähnte ich nachts eine Horde
schneepflückender Wesen zu sehen.
Ich griff in die Luft und fing die Kälte.

Hier im hohlen Leib des Baums
überlebte ich die zähe
verzögerte Kälte des Frühjahrs,

hörte nachts die dünne Geistermusik
und fand am Morgen einen Vorrat
von harten Kernen verdichteten Lebens.

Ich schloss die Augen, meditierte,
sah durch die Rinde die Welt
und fühlte mich schuldig.

Ich schloss die Augen
und sah die hellfarbenen Pflugochsen
über die Frühlingsfelder schreiten.

Ich hörte das dumpfe Brüllen und schüttelte
den nassen Lehm aus den Haaren.

I opened that bark door
and entered the tree.
The door closed with a rustling sound.

Motionless I sat in the cavern.
Spirits, of drifting snow,
visited me at night
with a clangour of gongs and a din of drums.

I swallowed wind and dew,
scarcely daring to breathe.

Or they whispered magical sayings,
they touched me.
I felt them, we sat knee to knee.
I lived in dank uncertainty.

At times by night I imagined I saw
a band of snow-plucking creatures.
I clutched at air and seized the cold.

Here in the tree's hollow body
I survived the obstinate
lingering coldness of spring,

at night heard the thin spirit music
and in the morning found a store
of hard kernels, solidified life.

I closed my eyes, meditated,
saw the world through the bark
and felt guilty.

I closed my eyes
and saw the pale plough oxen
cross the spring fields.

I heard their muted roar and shook
the wet clay out of my hair.

Ich schloss die Augen
und sah die Tochter des Salzhändlers
mit silberner Sichel
das Laub vom Maulbeerbaum schneiden.

Sie trug im Korb
das Seidenraupenfutter in die Kammer.

Ich schloss die Augen,
es kamen zwei Knechte,
sie legten die Säge an den Baum
und töteten mich.

KÖNIG LEAR

Unter dem Steinbruch
kommt er herauf,
den Jodlappen
um die rechte Hand gewickelt.

In elenden Dörfern
schlug er Knüppelholz
für seine Linsensuppe.

Jetzt kehrt er
im dürren Schatten
zerrissener Wolken
zu seiner Krone
in die Schlucht zurück.

I closed my eyes
and saw the salt merchant's daughter
with her silver sickle
lop the leaves of the mulberry tree.

In a basket she carried
the silkworm food into her room.

I closed my eyes,
two labourers came,
applied their saw to the tree
and killed me.

KING LEAR

At the quarry's edge
he comes walking up,
the iodine rag
wrapped round his right hand.

In poor villages
he cut knotty wood
for his lentil soup.

Now in the dry shadow
of torn clouds
he returns
to his crown
in the glen.

IM KALMUSGERUCH dänischer Wiesen
liegt immer noch Hamlet
und starrt in sein weisses Gesicht,
das im Wassergraben leuchtet.

Das letzte Wort
blieb ungesagt,
es schwamm auf dem Rücken der Biber fort.
Keiner weiss das Geheimnis.

TODTMOOS

In Todtmoos
sah ich in weisser leuchtender Schneeluft
schneepflückende Wesen fliegen.
Ich griff in den Flockenfall
und fing nur Kälte.

Schneenarben an den Felsen,
Wegzeichen wohin? Schriftzeichen,
nicht zu entziffern.

DER FREMDE geht davon
und hat den Stempel
aus Regen und Moos
noch rasch der Mauer aufgedrückt.
Eine Haselnuss im Geröll
blickt ihm mit weissem Auge nach.

Jahreszeiten, Missgeschicke, Nekrologe—
unbekümmert geht der Fremde davon.

IN THE RUSH ODOUR of Danish meadows
still Hamlet lies
staring into his white face
that gleams in the water ditch.

The last word
remains unspoken,
it swam off on the backs of beavers.
Nobody knows the secret.

TODTMOOS

At Todtmoos
in white shining snow air I saw
snow-plucking creatures fly.
I clutched at the falling flakes
and seized only coldness.

Snow scars on the rock,
trail markings to where? Glyphs,
indecipherable.

THE STRANGER leaves
and in parting quickly
has impressed the stamp
of rain and moss
upon the wall.
A hazelnut in the scree
follows his going with a white eye.

Seasons, mishaps, obituaries—
untroubled the stranger leaves.